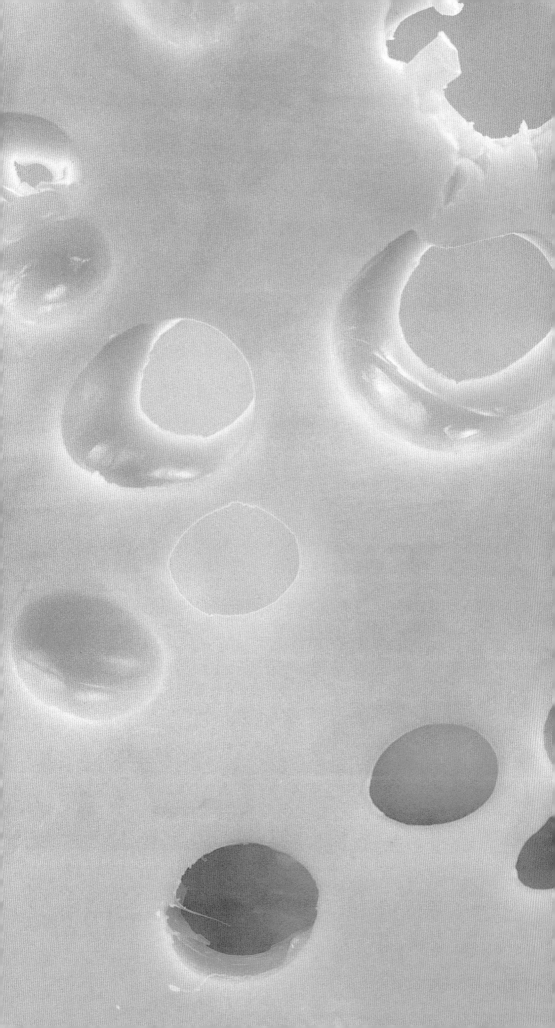

the
cheese
handbook

Bob Farrand

Executive Editor: Polly Manguel
Editors: Sharyn Conlan and Jo Lethaby
Proof-readers: Joanna Smith and Linda Doeser

Creative Director: Keith Martin
Executive Art Editor: Geoff Fennell
Freelance Designer: Justine Harrison

Picture Researcher: Rosie Garai
Production Controller: Lisa Moore
Indexer: Hilary Bird

Photographer: Ian Wallace
Home Economist: Oona van den Berg
Stylist: Antonia Gaunt
Contributing Recipe Author: Oona van den Berg

Other photography acknowledgements: Octopus Publishing Group Limited/
Sean Myers page 128/Philip Webb page 121.

The author would like to acknowledge the use with kind permission of the paneer recipe
on page 77 which is taken from Yamuna Devi's *The Art of Indian Vegetarian Cooking*
by Century Press and reprinted in *Good Cheese* magazine.

The Cheese Handbook by Bob Farrand

An Hachette Livre UK Company
www.hachettelivre.co.uk

First published in 2000 by Hamlyn, an imprint of Octopus Publishing Group Limited
2–4 Heron Quays, London E14 4JP
www.octopusbooks.co.uk

A CIP record for this book is available from the British Library

ISBN-13: 978-0-600-60062-6

10 9 8 7 6 5 4

Printed and bound in China

Notes

Standard level spoon measurements are used in all recipes.
1 tablespoon = one 15 ml spoon
1 teaspoon = one 5 ml spoon

Both metric and imperial measurements have been given in all recipes. Use one set of measurements
only and not a mixture of both.

Eggs should be medium unless otherwise stated.

Do not re-freeze a dish that has been frozen previously.

Ovens should be preheated to the specified temperature – if using a fan assisted oven, follow the
manufacturer's instructions for adjusting the time and temperature.

contents

introduction

One of my earliest memories is standing on tip-toe as a young child in the larder at home, stretching up for a wedge of Cheddar, and the intense pleasure of finally biting into the rich, firm, yellow cheese. It appears that a strange love of cheese has been a part of my life almost from the beginning.

The north Dorset market town of Shaftesbury where I was raised is more famous for Gold Hill, the familiar cobbled road and ancient Roman wall, than for cheese. We lived close to the foot of the hill and each morning the trip to school, and then later to work in the High Street, involved the seemingly endless trek up this incredibly steep slope to 'the top of the world'. Mr Perrott's High Class Provisioners at the far end of the High Street was where the town's genteel classes purchased their groceries during the early 1960s. He was by no means an accomplished businessman – it is doubtful he ever made money from his store, although his lack of business acumen was compensated by a deep appreciation of farmhouse cheeses, and an eccentric theatrical style of service that cajoled customers into sharing his passion.

As the 'boy' working in the store during school holidays, I was fostered in an appreciation of the seasonal changes found in farmhouse cheeses and the rich variation in flavours of Cheddars made on different days of the week using different starters. Part of my role was to remember which days' making each customer preferred and deliver their wedge to the counter as Mr Perrott performed his highly animated presentation. Few customers left the shop empty handed, nor would he allow them to buy cheese without first learning of its full heritage. In four years, my childhood preference for a mouthful of Cheddar was transformed by Mr Perrott into a life-long passion, coupled with a desire to share it with anyone prepared to join me in a cheese board.

Almost no logical selection criteria have been used in assembling the various cheeses in this book. Many feature regularly on our cheese boards at home and are much loved, others are constant reminders of long-remembered and enjoyed occasions. Many are not even personal favourites, but in our travels they feature prominently in tastings by virtue of popular demand, and several are included as mainstays in cooking or for buffets. All are better for a little time and trouble in selecting, a benefit which I sincerely hope each reader will quickly appreciate.

Understanding Cheese Types

The following is a useful guide to the five main cheese families, but you will frequently come across cheeses that do not fit neatly into any single category. Part of the fascination is its seemingly endless ability to surprise us with different styles. To my knowledge, there is no other food type that offers such a wide diversity of textures and flavours; certainly not meat nor baked goods.

1. Very Hard Cheeses (Brine Dipped)

Very hard cheeses are often referred to as cooked and pressed cheeses and form the group made from milk which is heat treated (but frequently not pasteurized) before renneting. The curds are scalded in the whey at a high temperature, pressed over a long period and, finally, salted and immersed in brine. These are mainly Continental cheeses which are very low in moisture and will therefore take many months, in some cases years, to mature fully. Cheeses falling into this category include Parmesan, Gruyère and Emmental. Variations within this family can sometimes serve to confuse, but the principal differences relate to whether the curd is cooked in the whey prior to being moulded, the temperature at which the curds are scalded, the pressure applied to the cheese in the mould and the salting techniques.

2. Hard Pressed Cheeses

Usually close in texture and firm in body, hard pressed cheeses are also referred to as pressed uncooked cheeses. In the UK, they form the most popular family of table cheeses. The starter is added to cooled milk, the curds are scalded at a medium temperature, around 42°C (107.6°F), and the curds are dry salted before the cheese is hard pressed in the mould to expel the moisture. This class of cheese includes many traditional British cheeses, such as Cheddar, which can be eaten from 3–24 months and older, and hard regional cheeses like Double Gloucester, which takes up to 12 months to mature. The general rule of thumb is the less moisture present in the cheese, the longer it takes to mature. These cheeses have good keeping qualities and their flavours intensify the longer they mature.

Some other cheeses in this family are scalded at a lower temperature, around 35°C (95°F), and then lightly pressed. These include British territorial cheeses known as 'crumblies' because they are difficult to cut without crumbling; they include Cheshire, most Lancashire cheeses and Wensleydale. They are slightly more open in texture than the other hard pressed cheeses and there is more moisture present, so the time taken to mature is less, generally 2–4 months.

3. Blue Cheeses

This large group is almost entirely semi-hard in texture. Most are not pressed and dry salted, though a few are very lightly pressed. Blue cheeses mature through a process where the curd develops a blue veining following the introduction of mould spores (*Penicillium roquefortii*) which break down the paste to develop fuller flavours. The spores are introduced at the start of cheesemaking and stainless steel rods pierce the cheese during maturation to allow air to penetrate and the mould to develop. Some blue cheeses, such as blue Bries, combine two types of mould – a surface mould and an internal blue mould. In terms of maturation time, treat these as you would a semi-hard cheese. They reach maturity from 3–8 months.

4. Mould-ripened Soft Cheeses

These are generally unpressed, so they have a higher moisture content and the ripening time is relatively short, in most cases 4–8 weeks. The curd is cut into larger pieces than for hard cheese and is not scalded, so more whey is retained. The surface-ripened cheeses include all Bries and Camemberts, which mature with the aid of a surface mould (*Penicillium camemberti*) which works its way towards the centre of the cheese. This creates a bloomy white rind and the chalky line in the centre of a Brie indicates where the ripening process has reached. A fully mature cheese will be creamy throughout. When young, the aroma is fresh, earthy, almost like the underside of a raw field mushroom, but as the cheeses approach full maturity, they develop an aroma redolent of boiled cabbage. These cheeses must never be allowed to develop the pungent aroma of ammonia.

The other cheeses within this category are washed rind or soft, drained cheeses, such as Port Salut, Pont l'Evêque and Livarot. Characterized by an orange-brown exterior, they are frequently washed in brine, wine or herbs to develop a bacterial culture which helps to mature the cheese but also develops a pungent smell that belies a milder, creamy, subtle flavour. High moisture in these cheeses means quick maturation and a shorter period when they are at their best and perfect for eating.

5. Fresh Cheeses

These cheeses generally have less initial acidity, producing a soft curd, and are not scalded to expel the whey and therefore have a high moisture content. They are as best on the day they are made and deteriorate very quickly. Many are so soft they must be moulded into small portions to preserve their shape and are sold in boxes, bags or foil. The best-known examples are Mozzarella and cream cheese.

The Cheesemaking Process

The first decision for the cheesemaker is the choice of milk. The type of animal is of singular importance in the creation of flavour, as is the breed – some produce a richer milk than others. The feed, the time of year, the age of the animal and the stage of her lactation cycle all impact on the final flavour and the cheesemaker's art is an ability to compensate for constant changes in the character of the milk. The best milk for Cheddar, for example, is drawn from cows during spring and summer, but blue cheeses are generally better from late summer and autumn milk. The perfect Vacherin Mont d'Or, however, demands milk from cows fed on winter hay to achieve its glory. The milk used may be full cream, partially skimmed, fully skimmed or have additional cream added, and may be a combination of morning and evening milk, the latter being slightly richer as a result of the day's feeding patterns.

Pasteurization and coagulation

Most cheesemakers pasteurize their milk at 72°C (161.6°F) for 15 seconds, a process that kills almost all bacteria present. Pasteurization continues to raise the hackles of purists, but cheeses made using unpasteurized milk are increasingly subjected to labelling more appropriate to cigarette packets. Pasteurization kills good and bad bacteria alike and most of the complex flavours found in cheeses made from unpasteurized milk so beloved by connoisseurs are a result of these bacteria. In an environment where food standards are increasingly more concerned with food hygiene rather than the quality of the food, the future for cheeses made from unpasteurized milk remains uncertain.

After pasteurization, a starter culture similar to that used in the making of yogurt is added to the milk. This sours the milk by converting the lactose into lactic acid. At this stage, the spores of the bacteria *Penicillium roquefortii* are added to the milk if it is being used to make blue cheese. Also at this stage annatto, an orange dye, is added to colour cheeses, such as Double Gloucester or Red Leicester.

Next, rennet is gently mixed with the milk, which begins to coagulate about 10 minutes later. These days, most British cheeses are made using vegetarian rennet in preference to animal rennet, which is an enzyme extracted from the stomach of a calf or goat. Lactic cheeses are coagulated without rennet, merely relying on lactic acid or sometimes the addition of lemon juice to separate the milk.

Cutting the curd

The set coagulum is cut into small pieces of curd with specially designed knives. This has the effect of releasing the whey, or liquid. Most of the protein, fat, vitamin A and much of the calcium in the milk remain in the curd, while a large part of the lactose and B vitamins are lost in the whey as it drains away. Deciding when to cut the set coagulum is one of the most time-sensitive decisions taken by the cheesemaker. Cut too soon and the soft curd is easily broken, leading to a loss of fat and protein in the whey and therefore a lower yield. Cut too late, when the curd is too firm, and it becomes difficult to cut into small pieces, leaving moisture trapped within it.

The size of curd cubes varies with different types of cheese. Hard, drier cheeses, such as Cheddar, are cut to the size of peas but semi-hard cheeses, such as Caerphilly and Wensleydale are cut to the size of cherries. The curd for soft cheeses is hardly cut at all as the moisture is retained within the cheese. The curds are also stirred to prevent the hardening of the coating which would restrict moisture release.

Scalding the curd

Ten minutes after cutting, the vat is heated to raise the temperature of the curds and whey which causes the protein strands to contract. The higher the temperature, the more moisture is squeezed out; and the smaller the curd particles, the quicker is the release of whey. Thus cheeses that are scalded to a temperature around 55°C (130°F), such as Gruyère, Emmental and Parmesan, are firmer in body than those that receive a low scald, such as Cheshire or Wensleydale, Cheddar, Gloucester, Leicester and Derby, are scalded at a medium temperature, around 42°C (107.6°F). Soft cheeses are not scalded at all.

The next stage is the most important in attaining the final moisture and firmness of the cheese. The curds and whey are stirred after scalding for a set period of time – Cheshire for 30–40 minutes, Cheddar for 50–60 minutes. The curd continues to shrink and release moisture, becoming firmer and drier. The curds and whey are stirred until the desired acidity and texture are reached. The stirring is stopped and the curd is allowed to settle on the bottom of the vat. At this point the whey is drawn off.

Processing the curd

For hard and semi-hard cheeses, the curd is subsequently cut or broken, piled and turned. These operations vary in duration according to the variety of cheese, but the cutting or breaking of the curd into smaller pieces increases surface area so whey is released at a faster rate and cooling is more rapid. Piling the curd blocks improves the release of whey, keeps the curd warm, encourages acid development and consolidates and conditions the curd texture. The curd is then milled into smaller pieces, promoting further removal of whey. Dry salt is added to traditional British cheeses at this stage to help shrink the curd and stimulate the release of more whey. This is known as mellowing, and the salt also acts as a preservative and contributes to the final flavour and texture of the cheese.

Pressing and maturing

Most hard cheeses are produced by pressing the curd in a mould for varying amounts of time. Farmhouse producers use cylindrical moulds the size of which are traditional to particular types of cheese. After pressing, the cheeses are bandaged, stored on shelves and turned daily at first and then weekly throughout the maturation time. Not all varieties of cheese are pressed, however. Some, such as Caerphilly and Wensleydale, are semi-pressed, and others, such as Stilton, Brie and Camembert, are not pressed at all. Once removed from the press, traditional cylindrical cheeses are bandaged in calico or muslin to maintain shape and are then covered in lard, waxed or dusted with flour to provide further protection and improve appearance. Modern block cheeses are wrapped in plastic film which acts as a rind. Cheeses such as Dutch Edam are treated with hot water, stained with red dye and coated in wax.

Some cheeses, such as Parmesan, are floated in brine for 21 days after moulding, which causes salt to be absorbed by the cheese to improve the flavour. The surface of the cheese develops into a hard dry rind which acts as a protection against bacteria growing on the surface during storage.

For cheeses with a white, bloomy mould, the curd is cut into small cubes and the curds and whey are ladled into round moulds where they drain for almost a day. The basic cheese shape has now been formed and cheeses are removed from their moulds and are salted, dried and sprayed with the bacteria *Penicillium candidum* or *camemberti*. The cheeses are left to ripen as the mould develops like thin white strands of grass. Washed rind cheeses, such as Pont l'Evêque and Livarot, are regularly wiped with brine during maturation which reacts with the rind to accelerate the maturation and give a richer flavour.

Special cases

The texture of cottage cheese is achieved by the slow heating of the curd before washing and draining. A cream dressing is normally added to give flavour. Mozzarella and Provolone, the *pasta filata* (stretched-curd) cheeses, are made by stretching the curd in warm water before moulding. Ricotta is made from whey to which whole milk is added. Heat causes the proteins to coagulate (acid may be added to help this) and rise to the surface; these are then drained and packaged.

Control Systems

There are systems to help preserve the integrity of certain cheeses and other foods produced within specific regions. The regulations in France, Appellation d'Origine Contrôlée (AOC), Spain, Denominacion de Origen (DO) and Italy, Denominazione di Origine Controllatta (DOC) have existed for some time, but in the last few years, the EU has created the Product of Designated Origin (PDO) system to protect specific foods made within the community boundaries.

The systems in France, Spain and Italy closely govern every aspect of cheese production. The locality, the type of milk and frequently the breed of cattle are all strictly controlled, as are the techniques of making and maturing. In some instances, even the time of the year during which a particular cheese can be made is controlled. The UK has been slower to protect its cheese heritage and until recently, only Stilton has been governed by any controls. This perhaps explains why English Territorial cheeses are now copied throughout the UK and beyond, and are mostly produced in large factories where the intrinsic character of each cheese has all but disappeared.

The recent introduction of PDO's has offered fresh opportunities to British cheesemakers to safeguard farmhouse cheeses. Apart from Stilton, which can be made only in the counties of Leicestershire, Nottinghamshire and Derby, there is now protection for West Country Farmhouse Cheddar which has been awarded a PDO.

In order to fulfil the the criteria laid down by the rules of the PDO, West Country Farmhouse Cheddar must be made on a farm in Cornwall, Devon, Dorset or Somerset and other than in exceptional circumstances, must use milk from cows grazing in those counties. The techniques for handling the curd during the cheesemaking process clearly stipulate it must always be turned and piled by hand and not by machine. The UK boasts some nine PDO cheeses at the time of writing, but others have applied for protection although we still lag well behind France, Spain and Italy.

Everyone with a passion for cheese should applaud and support the work of these controlling bodies. Look out for the designations marked on the cheeses indicating they are either AOC, DO, DOC or PDO. Not only will you be supporting the survival of regional characteristics in good cheese, you will almost certainly be rewarded with better flavours.

Planning a Cheese Board

Most large supermarkets currently pay scant attention to training; they prefer customers to help themselves from the pre-pack counter. To select cheese in perfect condition, you must first know when and how it was made. Unfortunately, most cheese counter staff are unable to provide this information, so avoid shops where the management fails to train its staff professionally.

There are five families of cheese and each achieves maturity over different time scales. The more moisture in a cheese, the quicker it matures. Harder cheeses always ripen over longer periods. A four-month Cheddar will almost certainly fail to please, whereas a Roquefort at the same age will likely be superb. Each cheese family matures at its own pace to develop its characteristic flavour and it pays to appreciate this when buying.

Planning the cheese board should occupy the cook for the same amount of time as organizing the main course or dessert – the cheese board is a course in its own right. Invest in the largest, most attractive board or plate you can afford and remember that providing one cheese knife is at least three too few.

A perfect balance

We all taste with our eyes first – colour, shape and texture are what initially attract us to food. Your cheeses should mirror this, with a studied balance of deep yellow wedges, rich orange-brown squares, slices of ivory-white paste pitted with deep greeny-blue veins, and dusty white globes. Pay no attention to the absurdities of food writers who proclaim the perfect cheese board comprises one superb example of a farmhouse cheese in perfect condition. The minimum number is four cheeses for a half-decent cheese board; we rarely venture below six.

Since the early 1980s, despite the growth in output of factory-made cheeses, there has been a massive renaissance in good artisan cheesemaking throughout Europe. The UK alone can now boast over 400 different cheeses, so there is no shortage of fascinating new ones to try. Work on the basis that each guest will like only two cheeses on your board, or three if you are lucky. Select an eclectic range of textures and flavours, from the mild and unassuming to the assertive cheeses that announce their arrival long before the first morsel is tasted. Make sure you include cheeses made using goats' and ewes' milk as well as cows'. Try each one before you buy and ensure you know their provenance and feel comfortable about their maturity. If necessary, sniff, poke and squeeze – you're the customer and you want the best. Buy just sufficient for the number of guests; better to leave them wanting more than to find yourself with a large slice of over-ripe Brie on the following day.

Experiment to the full, always including two new cheeses as this will add to the pleasure – particularly if you find local cheeses that few of your friends are likely to have previously encountered. On occasions through this book, you will find suggestions for wines to accompany certain cheeses. Take this as a loose guide only because it is dangerous both to the liver and the purse to attempt to serve the appropriate wine with each of six different cheeses. Far better to serve a single wine in contrast to the wines served before and after.

Preparing the cheese board

Prepare your cheese board early. If you have bought your cheeses from a supermarket, be conscious that they will have been stored at a very low temperature. The law requires shops to store cheese at below 8°C (45°F), although most supermarket delicatessen counters are much closer to 0°C (32°F), which is highly injurious to all cheese. Few houses are built with larders these days, so a cool garage in winter is fine for hard cheeses, but you may need to resort to the refrigerator in summer. Wrap all cheeses well, preferably in wax paper or foil, and store in the warmest part of the refrigerator.

Remove from refrigeration a good two hours before serving and tidy each cheese for display. Lay them on the board and cover with a clean tea towel to prevent drying out. In summer, select a cool corner to store until ready to serve.

Serving the cheese

The French and Italians love bread with their cheese, the British prefer biscuits and fruit – particularly ripe pears and crisp sharp apples. The fresh acidity in the fruit provides a perfect counter-balance to the richness of the cheese and while there's not a single shred of evidence in support of the theory, I have long maintained that fruit helps break down some of the fat in the cheese.

In mainland Europe, the cheese board appears after the main course and before pudding. In the UK, the cheese board is attacked after diners have devoured trolley-loads of tirimasu, chocolate gâteaux and spotted dick. Please yourself, but cheese precedes pudding in our house every time. But then we did give up desserts some 20 years ago.

cheese directory
12–105

Appenzell(er)

Switzerland

This is quite possibly Switzerland's oldest cheese, originating in the Canton of Appenzell in the 8th century. Records dating from the 12th century record a cheese from Appenzell made as a tithe payment to the Saint Gall monastery.

Now made in St Gallen, Thurgau and Zürich, Appenzeller is made using unpasteurized cows' milk. Its yellowish-brown rind is the result of regular washing with a brine marinade of herbs, spices and frequently wine or cider. This washing helps develop flavour in the dense, springy paste, which is occasionally pitted with small, pea-sized 'eyes'. At four to five months the aroma can be quite offensive. The flavour is strong and tangy, with a long creamy, fruity finish that lends itself well to fondues, salads and the cheese board.

Some years ago, the explorer Tim Severin sailed across the Atlantic in a leather boat in an attempt to recreate the supposed discovery of America by the Irish monk, St Brendan. He ate modern foods for the first half of the journey and was ill and weak. But with a diet of Appenzeller, grains and smoked, salted meats typical of the 6th century provided by TV chef, Glynn Christian, he thrived. What does that tell us about modern eating habits?

region
St Gallen, Thurgau and Zürich

milk
unpasteurized cows' milk

style
semi-hard wheels with natural rind

taste
strong, tangy, with a long creamy, fruity finish

England

Smoked cheeses are often a disappointment. Fish is easy to smoke since its thin, light texture allows flavour to permeate through the flesh. Smoking cheese, on the other hand, is frequently less successful because the dense texture prevents the smoke from penetrating to the heart of the cheese. This leads to an intense smokiness on the outside and an imbalance of flavour inside, which many people find unsatisfactory.

Applewood Smoked appears to have solved the problem, although the mere mention of its name to many cheese purists is sufficient to cause them a fit. The makers start with English mature Cheddar, which is milled before the addition of a liquid smoke concentrate. The mixture is repressed and washed in paprika to create the illusion of a genuine smoked Cheddar.

Applewood exchanges the firm, open texture of proper Cheddar in favour of a smoother feel and an evenly distributed smoky flavour, which for more than 35 years has earned the Ilchester Cheese Company a considerable fortune. Purists still pour scorn on it, but consumers continue to enjoy it. That alone justifies its inclusion in this book.

If you happen to be more of a purist, there are properly smoked Cheddars around but you will need to search a little harder. Those from Quickes or Sturminster Newton are unlikely to disappoint.

region
West Country

milk
pasteurized cows' milk

style
semi-hard, dark orange disc

taste
smoky

Ardrahan
Ireland

The UK Cheese Guild's relationship with Irish cheesemakers began in 1988 at the first London International Cheese Competition. The day of the judging coincided with the England–Ireland rugby international at Twickenham and several cheesemakers deposited their cheeses for judging en route to the ground. It was then that we learned the essential ingredient for Irish farmhouse cheese is the personality of the cheesemaker. Each cheese reflects the character of the person who made it.

Where better to start than Kanturk in County Cork, home to the late Eugene Burns and his widow Mary and their pedigree herd of Friesians? Ardrahan is a washed rind cheese, which starts life as a smooth, round, pure white wheel, but when fully matured at around eight weeks is wrinkled and pale orange-brown.

Several Irish farmhouse cheeses boast a pronounced earthy aroma, few more so than Ardrahan, but allow yourself time to grow accustomed to it. At its best, the yellow paste is creamy right through to the centre with a random scattering of holes. I have read several attempts at describing the flavours but none does it justice. There is salt and butter and mushroom, but you can never be sure with Ardrahan as each cheese is just a touch different from the last. You are better off tasting it for yourself each time you buy it.

region
County Cork

milk
pasteurized cows' milk

style
semi-hard, washed rind disc

taste
salty, buttery and mushroomy

Austrian Smoked

Austria

Many of us are familiar with one Austrian cheese, the processed smoked variety seen in supermarket self-service cabinets in countless shapes, sizes and flavours. The majority are chubby, brown sausage shapes, many in individual portions, and include ham, celery, onion and many other flavours.

Originally, these were made by smoking the milk before cheesemaking, but these days, young Austrian smoked Emmental is processed to prolong its life and arrest further development of its flavour. Austrian Smoked in all its guises has sustained several million children's lunch boxes, including my own, for years and they are a deal more wholesome than the chemically saturated processed cheese slices fed to youngsters these days.

Austria can lay claim to a more traditional heritage with Bergkäse (mountain cheese; *see below*), made using both Emmental and Gruyère recipes in the western tip of the country. The milk is unpasteurized and the herds are small. Cows spend their springs and summers in the mountains, while the valleys produce hay for winter feed, which means that no cow cake or silage is used, which would taint the natural flavours of the milk.

Farmers quite literally carry the finished cheeses down the mountain on their backs – no doubt an inducement to keep things on a small scale. Even after lengthy maturation, Bergkäses are never overpowering, always creamy rich with the flavour of fresh grass and a lingering nuttiness.

region
Austrian Alps

milk
unpasteurized cows' milk

style
semi-hard, cooked, similar to Emmental and Gruyère

taste
creamy rich with a fresh and nutty flavour

Banon
France

My first encounter with a good mature Banon outside France was some years ago in Mitcham, south London, a far cry from its roots in Provence. Immediately recognizable by its characteristic jacket of chestnut leaves wrapped around a small, disc-shaped cheese tied in a parcel with raffia, the Banon I tasted had travelled overnight in the boot of a well-known cheese wholesaler's car from a farm a few kilometres outside the market town of Banon itself. He was justifiably pleased with himself.

The chestnut leaves are not merely decoration, they are soaked in wine or eau de vie, as is the cheese itself in many versions. As it ages, delicately coloured mould develops on the surface of the cheese as it draws intensive flavours from the leaves. Some claim that when young and soft, the cheese is uncomfortably acidic, almost redolent of Muscadet. If matured well, however, to about seven weeks or so, it develops far more interesting and complex flavours.

Such was the experience in south London – rich, vegetal, fruity and highly piquant with an ability to make you pucker; not for the fainthearted. Select with care – almost every example found in the UK is too young, and sadly, it is rarely a cheese you are able to taste before you buy. Give it a gentle squeeze – it needs to be soft and pliable with the merest hint of cheese breaking through the leaves but no trace of a smell of ammonia. A reputable cheesemonger will understand what you're doing.

Nowadays, Banon is made in factories, small dairies and on farms and you will find varieties made from goats', sheep's and cows' milk and occasionally even a combination. Those made in factories and available in the UK, however, are mostly made from pasteurized cows' milk.

region
Provence

milk
cows', goats' or sheep's milk

style
semi-soft, small disc,
wrapped in leaves

taste
rich, vegetal, fruity
and highly piquant

Beenleigh Blue

England

region
Totnes, Devon

milk
unpasteurized sheep's milk

style
semi-hard, cylindrical blue

taste
creamy, rich and complex

If I had to choose the single luxury item I could take to a desert island, as on the BBC radio programme *Desert Island Discs*, my choice would be Beenleigh Blue. Its creator, Robin Congdon, and his partner, Sarie Cooper, are arguably the UK's most gifted cheesemakers. Robin began experimenting with unpasteurized sheep's milk blue cheeses in 1982 in the Dart Valley near Totnes in Devon. It took almost six years of trial and error before he was satisfied with his efforts.

A local flock of Dorset and Friesian cross sheep provides the milk, and each stage of cheesemaking is controlled according to the time of year, temperature, humidity and condition of the milk. The result is a foil-wrapped cheese, which matures for up to nine months into a moist, crumbly paste with occasional tiny holes. The flavours are creamy rich and complex, with strong floral tones balancing the sweetness of the sheep's milk and just a hint of the sea.

Robin refuses to use frozen milk during the period when the ewes are lambing, so sadly the cheese is not available from February until late summer. As a result, always taste before buying. Some small cheese shops sell in such small quantities that you will occasionally find examples that are tired and dry and not pleasant.

Another of the couple's blue cheeses is Devon Blue, an alternative to Stilton but made using unpasteurized cows' milk. Matured in four months, it lacks the mouth-puckering assertiveness of Stilton. Harbourne Blue is a goats' milk blue, which at around seven months develops a smooth texture and grassy characteristics, which avoid any unpleasant 'goatiness'.

recipe using Harbourne Blue, see page: 130

Bel Paese

Italy

region
Lombardy

milk
pasteurized cows' milk

style
soft and creamy, small wheel
or tiny disc

taste
mild, delicate, slightly
sweet flavour

Dante once described Italy as 'bel paese' – beautiful country – and few have dared argue with his description since. In 1906, a Lombardy cheesemaker called Egidio Galbani created a sweet, buttery cheese, pale yellow in colour, with a smooth springy texture and a shiny golden rind. He sought a name for his new cheese, convinced as he was that his invention would prove the key to his fortune. A family friend was the writer Abbot Antonio Stoppani, whose book *Bel Paese* provided Galbani with the necessary inspiration, and so began the story of a successful cheese and a company that today ranks as one of the world's largest cheesemakers.

Egidio Galbani has always paid homage to the source of his inspiration; to this day, Stoppani's portrait imposed on a map of his beloved Italy appears on the foil wrapping of every Bel Paese made in Europe. A similar cheese is made under licence in the USA.

Bel Paese is an uncooked, lightly pressed cows' milk cheese, which matures for between one and three months to give a mild, delicate, slightly sweet flavour, which is as uncomplicated to enjoy as a table cheese as it is when used in cooking. If you buy it from a delicatessen, the cheese will be a larger 2 kg (4 lb) wheel, covered with a yellow wax.

recipes using Bel Paese, see pages: 137; 151

Bleu d'Auvergne
France

Traditional cheeses frequently reflect the character of the region in which they are made and Bleu d'Auvergne (AOC) is no exception. Often thought of as a cows' milk version of the Roquefort made close by, this is no imitation cheese. It is very much its own personality – a true reflection of the harsh but extraordinary beauty of the region

It is a foil-wrapped, cylindrical cheese with a thin, moist, pinkish skin. This hides a paste, which breaks down during three months maturation into steely grey-green holes that eventually encourage the cheese to collapse. Avoid cheeses that have broken down too much or are overly sticky on the outside.

The flavour is sharp, tangy and slightly salty, with a creamy consistency that should be light and melting on the tongue. The older the cheese, the spicier the finish.

Almost every example you find outside France is made of pasteurized cows' milk and these days, only a few dairies use raw milk. On a visit to Clermont Ferrand, the city after which my forefathers were named, I once found a cheese shop run by an *affineur* of great charm and enthusiasm. He sold me a slice of an unpasteurized Bleu d'Auvergne, which he had nurtured to perfect maturity. It lacked the intensive blueing of the pasteurized versions seen in the UK, but was infinitely more delicate and complex.

region
Auvergne

milk
cows' milk

style
semi-soft, small cylinder, blue

taste
rich, vegetal, fruity
and piquant

recipe using Bleu d'Auvergne, see page: 203

21

Brie
France

One year, at the London International Cheese Competition, a disgruntled cheesemaker approached me the day after the judging and emphatically argued that the winning Brie de Meaux was inferior to his cheese, which had been placed second. At the time of his complaint he was right, because so brief is the period when a Brie is perfect for eating, that the winning cheese, which was perfection on Saturday, was way past its best by Sunday afternoon.

Brie, in common with Camembert and Cheddar, has been borrowed by cheesemakers around the world, but in most instances has suffered in transit. Some good Bries are made in factories, many from pasteurized milk using special starters, which the makers claim can replicate the complex flavours of raw milk Bries. Some large manufacturers add extra cream for triple cream Bries and others make stabilized curd Bries with a uniform texture that needs no further maturation.

region
traditionally the Isle de
France, now almost
everywhere

milk
unpasteurized and
pasteurized cows' milk

style
soft, large flat disc

taste
mild and creamy to
mushrooms and
boiled cabbage

The West of England, Germany, Ireland and beyond all produce Bries in their own styles. Many are not bad, but nor are they truly memorable. It is to the Isle de France, some 50 km (31 miles) east of Paris that you need to travel for Bries that quicken the pulse.

Brie de Meaux is, in modern parlance, an awesome Brie, a benchmark by which all others are measured. AOC regulations prescribe that the cows' milk is unpasteurized, the curd is hardly cut and must be hand-ladled into moulds using special shovels. Traditionally, the cheesemaker hands the semi-ripe Brie over to an *affineur*, a professional maturer who nurtures the cheese to maturity. When young, a Brie has the aroma of raw mushroom, mild and earthy. Four weeks later, it is *à point* or at its best, and has the aroma of over-boiled cabbage while its velvety white exterior is now scattered with thin reddish-brown lines and patches.

The paste has lost its firm chalkiness and is bulging outwards from the heart of the cheese, straw coloured and even textured, but never runny. The flavours reflect the Brie's heritage: earthy, grassy, a hint of mushroom blending with a rich smokiness that unstintingly attacks every single taste bud.

Brie de Melun hails from the same region and is also subject to AOC regulations. Whereas milk for Brie de Meaux coagulates in 30 minutes using animal rennet, Brie de Melun uses lactic fermentation, which takes up to 18 hours. Maturation is also longer, involving constantly turning the cheeses for up to 10 weeks. The thin rind darkens with red-brown stains and a dusting of yellow mould. The flavour is unmistakably Brie but reminding us more of the dry salt used during the making.

Brie de Coulommiers is not AOC and you therefore find versions in supermarkets that disappoint. As a result of the slightly 'unclean' flavours that often characterize this cheese, it frequently struggles to please in the UK.

Final tips are to buy the best Brie you can afford and be conscious of when you intend to eat it. A fully ripe Brie will suffer if stored too long at low temperatures. If, on the other hand, you are buying on Thursday for eating on Sunday, select your Brie with some chalkiness remaining in the paste and bring it to perfection at home, preferably in a larder or similar cool place. Leave plenty of time for your Brie to reach room temperature and always refuse any that smells of ammonia.

recipes using Brie, see pages: 120; 126; 182

Cabrales

Spain

While judging at the London International Cheese Competition, a cheese grader once disparagingly commented that he was never sure what milk the Spanish used to make their cheeses. The truth is that Spanish cheesemakers have adapted to terrains less hospitable than the manicured pastures of rural England and have perfected the art of making cheese from whatever milk is available.

As if to prove the point, their most famous blue, the Cabrales and its twin brother, Picon or Picos de Europa, is best when made in spring and summer from the mixed milk of goat, sheep and cow. Winter cheeses are made only from cows' milk and are far less interesting.

Cabrales is made in northern Spain, in a region known as the Asturias. The farmers allow their animals to graze on rich mountain pastures during spring and summer and mature the raw milk blue cheese in natural limestone caves and cellars. Natural vents called *soplidos* feed a constant supply of cold, damp, saline-rich oxygen from the Atlantic into the caves, maintaining constant temperature and humidity. The blue penicillium mould develops naturally to create a cheese with a distinctively strong musty aroma of damp cellars, the texture of warm butter and a complexity of flavour that reflects each of the three different milks. The finish is long, spicy, assertive and mouth-puckering.

In common with all of Spain's classic cheeses, Cabrales is protected by a Denomination of Origin (DO).

region
Asturias

milk
unpasteurized cows' or sheep's milk

style
semi-hard blue wrapped either in maple leaves or foil

taste
spicy, assertive and mouth-puckering

Caerphilly

region
traditionally Caerphilly, but now anywhere

milk
pasteurized and unpasteurized cows' milk

style
semi-hard wheels of grey/white dust or white blocks

taste
crumbly, fruity and slightly salty

This least-known of British territorials has all but disappeared, surviving in a few isolated farms, none of which is in Caerphilly itself. Blocks of a white, crumbly cheese bearing the same name languish in supermarket chiller cabinets, but do not be misled. These are made in giant factories where the milk is drawn from a thousand farms and mixed to make a different British territorial each day of the week.

During a recent series of tutored tastings, we compared the Caerphilly from Gorwydd Farm in Tregaron with a prepacked Caerphilly purchased from a large supermarket in London. The factory cheese was crumbly and white with an initial hint of sourness on the tongue, which quickly faded to nothing.

Gorwydd Farm Caerphilly is made by cheesemaker Todd Trethowen, using unpasteurized milk. Each part of the cheesemaking process is conducted by hand and after settling the curds in moulds, the cheeses are soaked overnight in brine to seal in flavour and moisture.

At two and a half months, a good Caerphilly is light and crumbly with a terrific fruitiness. There is a hint of salt from the brine, which, as miners would testify, used to counteract the salt lost during a hard day's toil down the pit.

Only by this direct comparison between cheeses were our audiences in London able to appreciate the complexity that accompanies properly made cheeses. There are several farmhouse Caerphillys available – go seek them out and give a wide berth to anything wrapped in plastic in a chiller cabinet.

Cambozola
Germany

Wherever I travel to talk about cheese, I relate a little story about Cambozola. For the life of me I cannot recall where I originally heard it, nor am I entirely certain it's true – but it hardly matters.

During the late 1960s, a number of German cheesemakers sat around a table discussing the fact that there existed no German blue cheese to rival the great blues from other European nations. 'We shall invent one,' they agreed. So they created a new blue cheese. 'What shall we call it?' they asked at their next meeting. They gazed at their new cheese, realized it was white on the outside like a Camembert and blue on the inside like Gorgonzola so they merged the two names together to form Cambozola.

You may care little for the story but millions love the cheese. It sells all over the world and other cheesemakers continually seek to copy its style. The edible white rind encloses a marbled paste, which is smooth and rich in texture. Depending on the degree of ripeness, it varies in flavour from very mild and lactic to an unassuming spiciness – the complete antidote to everyone who swears they dislike blue cheese. Similar brands include Bavarian Blue, Blue Bayou and Paladin.

region
southern Germany

milk
pasteurized cows' milk

style
semi-soft, white flat disc, blue veining

taste
mild and creamy

recipe using Cambozola, see page: 164

Camembert
France

I proposed to my wife over the cheese course in a restaurant in St Malo in northern Brittany. The veritable Camembert de Normandie was as perfect as I had ever tasted, the Calvados was the intoxicating partner; truly a marriage made in heaven. What else could a cheese lover do other than cement the relationship?

Wherever you find cheese you find Camembert – or rather, a version of it. As ever, we shall initially concern ourselves with those that please most. The Camembert we know today is a relatively young cheese – having begun life in the late 18th century when, as the story goes, a Normandy farmer's wife, Mme Harel, gave shelter to a priest from the Brie region, east of Paris. Most small, round cheeses produced in Normandy at the time were covered with irregular red moulds but the priest showed Mme Harel how to mature cheese with the white flora moulds found on Bries.

Interestingly, it was not until around 1910 that Camembert came into its own, when the introduction of *Penicillium candidum* ensured a controlled development of the white mould on Camembert. A little earlier, the invention of the little round wooden boxes used to store Camembert contributed enormously to its spread in popularity. Have box, will travel – the original prepacked cheese.

Camembert de Normandie is the only AOC Camembert and the rules governing its manufacture are stringent. Only the unpasteurized milk from the indigenous Normandy cows may be used and the curd is never cut, merely sliced vertically. Four or five ladles of curd are poured by hand into each mould, with a resting period of at least 20 minutes between every pouring to allow the curd to settle.

region
traditionally Normandy, now almost everywhere

milk
unpasteurized and pasteurized cows' milk

style
soft, small flat disc

taste
mild and creamy to salty and fruity

Traditionally, this was undertaken only by women, generally considered more gentle than men, who might possibly treat the curd too roughly. Three years ago, I visited one of the largest co-operative producers of Camembert de Normandie where I witnessed this operation carried out by a robot. I am reliably informed the robot is female and exactly replicates the pouring action of a Normandy farmer's wife! Look for the words '*moulé à la louche*' on the box for assurance that ladling was properly undertaken, with or without the robot.

The cheese must be dry salted and maturation takes at least 21 days, depending on the time of year, temperature and so on. Individual preferences are important with Camembert. Many people in northern France prefer a chalky centre and milder flavour, others seek out the intensely creamy complexity of a cheese close to, but never quite, ammoniac. As the cheese approaches maturity, the pure white mould darkens with red lines, particularly around the edges, and when perfect, it gives a little but springs back into shape when gently squeezed between the thumb and forefinger. The prevailing aroma is of mushroom, as is the flavour, with real earthy tones, a hint of salt, herbs and a meaty texture.

Each country has its version of Camembert and many are far from uninteresting. Factory-made versions sell all over France, while in Germany, Italy, the UK and Ireland, Camembert-style cheeses abound. The versions made in Somerset are milder and more creamy than the French, like clotted cream meeting mushroom soup. The locals mostly prefer it to the imports from across the channel. Camembert is a versatile ingredient in a number of dishes and even an average specimen is much improved in cooking – try it deep-fried in breadcrumbs as a first course.

recipes using Camembert, see pages: 126; 182

Cantal
France

Be careful when choosing Cantal because it is a cheese of many personalities. When young, it is approachable, occasionally sharp and rarely well balanced. When older, you are dealing with a cheese that takes time to understand.

Cantal is the closest the French come to making Cheddar and it is their oldest cheese, predating the soft, mould-ripened cheeses for which they are famous by several thousand years. Like Cheddar, you find versions of this AOC cheese made in farmhouses, small dairies and in large creameries. There is a much-prized version, Cantal Fermier, or more commonly known as Salers, which is made by hand during the summer months in mountain chalets, where the farmers take their cattle to feed on the rich grasses and wild flowers of the high pastures.

When made on farms, the milk for Cantal is unpasteurized and if aged to six months, the rind darkens from yellow to grey and the paste becomes firm and dry. It has a nutty flavour, with a long-lingering acidity you need to become accustomed to. You may get some drying out on the rind, which results in cracks and the occasional streak of mould into the paste. Don't worry, it's a sign of a good cheese.

Factory versions use pasteurized milk and tend to be sold young – just over a month old. They are softer, moist cheeses that are rarely worth the effort.

region
Auvergne

milk
unpasteurized and
pasteurized cows' milk

style
hard, large cylinder

taste
mild and creamy to
salty and fruity with a
nutty finish

Cashel Blue
Ireland

This is in the modern style of blue cheeses, softer and more creamy than traditional British blues. Made in County Tipperary, where Jane and Louis Grubb first developed it in the late 1980s, Cashel Blue hits top form in December, when a 14-week cheese will have come from cows that grazed on rich, early autumn pastures. That's not to say that it doesn't please all year round, but you do need to take care over its maturity.

The Grubbs now pasteurize all the milk for Cashel Blue and the young round cheeses are wrapped in foil at two weeks to inhibit excessive mould development on the outside.

When the UK Cheese Guild first started working regularly in Ireland, Michael Horgan, an excellent cheese distributor, asked me to conduct tutored tastings with two Cashel Blues, one at around eight weeks old and the other at a full 14 weeks. The younger cheese is firm, sharp and lacking balance and definitely not to my taste. The older is soft, fondantly creamy and displays a subtle harmony between the buttery paste and the blue-grey veining.

Throughout two weeks of tasting, involving several hundred people, the verdict on the two Cashel Blues was evenly split – positive proof that there's no accounting for taste. Any leftovers make an excellent cheese and celery soup, regardless of their age.

region
County Tipperary

milk
pasteurized cows' milk

style
creamy, blue-veined, foil-wrapped cylinder

taste
creamy, sweet, with a salty finish

recipe using Cashel Blue, see page: 203

Chaource
France

In 1992, the UK Cheese Guild organized a cheese delicatessen at the BBC Good Food Show in Birmingham and spent four days introducing the British public to a basket full of relatively unfamiliar cheeses. A cylindrical white-mould cheese from the Champagne region called Chaource was the undisputed champion of the show. Almost everyone who encountered it fell under its spell.

Admittedly, they were tasting a young Chaource at just two weeks, when the rind is still furry white, the texture is chalky and the flavour is light, unobtrusively lactic and melts in the mouth like sorbet. We sold them by the lorry load.

If you are fortunate enough to find a Chaource with a dark yellow rind pitted with reddish-brown streaks, you are in for a different treat. The paste is then runny around the edges, with the consistency of clotted cream in the centre. The flavours have refined to a mushroomy nuttiness with background notes of grapes and a slight saltiness on the finish. It is well worth the wait. Purists recommend eating an older Chaource with a glass of Champagne. I tried it only once and quickly reverted to red Burgundy.

The AOC versions made in smaller dairies use unpasteurized milk, while the milk used for Chaource made in large creameries is pasteurized.

region
Borgogne and Champagne

milk
unpasteurized and
pasteurized cows' milk

style
semi-soft, small,
downy-white cylinder

taste
mushroomy nuttiness with
background of grapes and a
slight saltiness

Cheddar
England

Cheddar cheese was already in great demand by the reign of the first Queen Elizabeth of England. Farmers' wives eking out their meagre existences in the Mendip Hills near the Cheddar Gorge had long made hard cheese to preserve the protein in spring and summer milk for cold winter days. The soil, the grass, the breed of cattle and even the climate played a part in developing the unique characteristics of this cheese, which in 1655 was described as 'the best in England'.

The opening of the New World and subsequent mass emigration ensured that wherever cheese is made, you will find a variation of Cheddar. The name is unprotected and is frequently used generically to describe any cheese that is hard and yellow and almost always made in factories. The real stuff is firm, nutty, sweet and richly grassy, with a bite that lingers comfortably in the back of your throat. This kind of Cheddar can only be hand-made on farms in Devon, Cornwall, Dorset or Somerset and is subject to a European control in the form of a PDO.

Sadly, there are only a handful of traditional farmhouse Cheddar makers left. There are even fewer making Cheddar from unpasteurized milk. Tonnes of identical Cheddars made in highly automated factories and sold through supermarkets have persuaded the last two generations that good Cheddar possesses the characteristics of toilet soap.

Buying proper Cheddar is rarely easy and a little time and effort will pay delicious dividends. The genuine article should always be labelled 'West Country Farmhouse

region
worldwide, but originally the West Country

milk
unpasteurized and pasteurized cows' milk

style
hard, pale to deep yellow, cylinder or block

taste
mild and bland to rich, sharp and nutty

Cheddar' – mostly it should be prefixed with the word 'traditional'. Exercise caution over this last word, however. Its only meaning is to describe a round-shaped cheese; it has no bearing on the way the cheese has been made and many so-called 'traditional' cheeses are made in large factories.

Traditional cloth-bound Cheddars with a rind are generally the best, although several farms make block Cheddar in the old-fashioned way and some of it is very good. Wherever possible, buy from a retailer who provides you with the name of the farm. Keen, Montgomery, Quickes, Denhay, Chewton and Green are ones to seek out.

A good retailer will also tell you when the cheese was made. The best Cheddars are made from April through to early September, when the cows are outside, grazing on fresh grass and wild flowers. These Cheddars are superb at 12 months and those made from April to July can often be absolutely mind-blowing at 18 months – if you are lucky enough to find them. Winter Cheddars made from milk drawn from silage-fed cattle are rarely as interesting; they lack grassy notes and many display strong hints of fermented grass.

Do not be put off by lines of blue mould, which sometimes invade the cheese. Traditional West Country Cheddars are matured in the open air and not wrapped in plastic, so the odd hairline crack in the rind occasionally allows mould to penetrate the cheese. It hardly detracts from the taste, it certainly won't harm you and it is somewhat reassuring to know that human beings rather than machines made your Cheddar.

By far the majority of Cheddar consumed in the world is made in factories or creameries, and comparing them to Cheddars made by hand on farms in the West of England probably serves little purpose. Factory-made Cheddars achieve a consistent standard in much the same way as the French Vin de Pays wines – quaffable but rarely stunning. Farmhouse Cheddar, on the other hand, may sometimes disappoint when made during the winter months but mostly, they deliver a complex balance of flavours every bit as satisfying as a vintage claret.

recipes using Cheddar, see pages: 108; 111; 116; 122; 125; 136; 143; 160; 161; 172; 186

Cheshire
England

region
traditionally Cheshire
and Shropshire

milk
unpasteurized and
pasteurized cows' milk

style
crumbly, white or pale
orange, cylinder or block

taste
salty edge with a
crumbly freshness

England's oldest cheese was fed to Roman soldiers garrisoned at Chester and gets a mention in the Domesday Book, yet finding it in 21st-century Britain is close to impossible. Alex Williams, a good friend and long-established cheese retailer from Wem in Shropshire, assures me that the only place to buy proper Cheshire cheese is in the area of its birth. 'The best,' he says, 'never gets away.'

The good stuff is made in Cheshire and a short distance over the border into Shropshire, in the area below Nantwich and Middlewich. Heavy salt deposits in the soil yield a grass that creates milk with a higher salt content. The resulting cheese develops a characteristic salty edge and crumbly freshness that cannot be replicated anywhere else in the world. Sadly, the uniform slabs of cheese masquerading as Cheshire sold in most supermarkets are made in large factories from anonymous milk, and are wrapped in plastic for so long as to lose all of the cheese's crumbly texture.

Try a cloth-bound Hares Cheshire at six weeks and you will find it is fresh, curdy and salty. Mrs Appleby's unpasteurized coloured Cheshire will go to six months and beyond if it has been made slowly and carefully and will develop further richness and a distinctive tang. A fast-made cheese at that age would be harsh and acidic. Take no notice of the occasional green vein meandering through the cheese, it's your proof of authenticity. If you do see a Cheshire cheese for sale outside the UK, it will as often as not be called Chester, and it probably won't be any good either.

Chèvre
France

The street market close to the famous Colombe d'Or restaurant in St Paul de Vence, a few kilometres north of Nice, is just like a thousand similar markets throughout France. On a warm July morning in 1993, a farmer invited us to examine the small, round cheese he lifted from a wooden display on his stall. My wife glanced at the uneven pink and brown rind, noted the dirt under the farmer's fingernails, the Gauloise hanging from his lips and the absence of refrigeration, and enquired as to the name of the cheese. It had no name – it was just a Chèvre – and in spite of her qualms, she bought his cheese, which we ate and enjoyed and lived to tell the tale.

Not one cheese but a veritable family of cheeses that come in all shapes and sizes, Chèvre is the generic name for any goats' milk cheese that has no name of its own, and is often thought to be the heart of every French cheese board.

The most familiar is the Chèvre log, found in almost every supermarket and the cornerstone of the ubiquitous grilled goats' cheese salad. The colour is snow white, although sometimes covered in an edible black ash, and the texture is soft and grainy. Cheeses this young are mild, slightly salty, and clean and fruity in flavour. In France, some Chèvres are allowed to age into gnarled, wrinkled specimens, which become brittle in texture with a pronounced earthy, goat aroma and flavour. These are to be eaten with care and a full-bodied red wine.

region
all over France

milk
unpasteurized and
pasteurized goats' milk

style
semi-soft to rock hard,
small cylinder, log,
pyramid or disc

taste
mild to rich and tangy

recipes using Chèvre, see pages: 166; 180

Comté
France

Man, not nature, creates boundaries, which is why the cheeses made all around the Alps are remarkably similar. From the Bergkäses in Germany and Austria to Fontal in Italy and the Gruyères of France and Switzerland, all are of identical lineage, yet reflect the individual characteristics of regionality.

Gruyère de Comté (AOC) and the closely related Beaufort (AOC) are the ancient Gruyères of France and giants in the cheese world, sometimes weighing in at over 50 kg (110 lb). Made in summer, high up in the mountains, their size is a reflection of the need to make cheeses that mature well into winter, and the shape and weight is determined by the difficulty in transporting them down the mountains in autumn.

Comté has medium-sized holes or 'eyes', not as large as in Emmental, and if it's a really good specimen, an occasional drop of moisture, or 'tear', will be found in an eye. The texture is firm but smooth and the paste will crack open when cut. There is a distinctive nuttiness found in most Gruyères but in Comté, this combines with an almost fudge-like mouth feel with hints of wild alpine flowers, summer fruits and hay. Cheeses like these are perfect in picnics with salami, air-dried ham, the freshest bread and a robust red wine matured in oak.

region
Franche-Comté

milk
unpasteurized cows' milk

style
hard, large flat wheel

taste
distinctive nuttiness

recipe using Comté, see page: 111

Coolea
Ireland

High up in the remote hills west of Macroom in County Cork, Helen and Dick Willems created a Gouda-style cheese shortly after emigrating there from Holland in the early 1980s.

I really should come clean on Gouda because, apart from some exceptional long-matured versions, it leaves me cold – a cheese for those who don't really like cheese.

Coolea is different, as are most other Dutch-style cheeses made in Ireland. Perhaps it is a result of the endless supply of lush green pastures full of wild flowers untouched by intensive farming. Maybe, as I have suggested elsewhere, it is also to do with the character and integrity of individual farmhouse cheesemakers, as opposed to the anonymity of large factories.

The unpasteurized milk for Coolea is from the Willems' own herd of cattle, and the cheese develops with a hard orange-yellow rind protecting a rich yellow paste scattered with holes. At six months it is rich, sweet and grassy, but at twice that age it grows strong and buttery.

In Michaelstown in 1998, I was offered a taste from a stunning two-year-old 10 kg (22 lb) wheel with a flavour of such incredible intensity, I can recall it vividly even as I type these words.

region
County Cork

milk
pasteurized cows' milk

style
hard, thick disc

taste
rich, creamy and salty

Cornish Yarg

England

Tell most young people that Cornish Yarg is wrapped in nettle leaves and their faces invariably tighten into that expression that is the visual equivalent of disgusting. Offer them a taste and they become a picture of contentment.

Yarg is an attractive and easily appreciated cheese made by Lynher Dairies, using pasteurized milk from their own pedigree Friesian–Holstein cattle grazing on grasslands belonging to the Duchy of Cornwall. The curd is not scalded during cheesemaking, which results in a softer, open-textured cheese that draws just a hint of flavour from its unique coat of sterilized nettles. A young cheese at around six weeks is mild, fresh and lemony, but give it another fortnight or so and the paste softens as the flavour matures, and you have a unique vegetal blend of Cornish grass and old nettles mixed with top-of-the milk cream.

The dark, purple-grey nettle leaves with their intricately woven patterns add an extra dimension to the cheese board and you can amuse your dinner guests by telling them that Yarg is not an old Cornish dialect word but Alan Gray's surname spelt backwards. He was the cheesemaker who discovered a very ancient cheese recipe in his attic during the 1970s and decided to give it a try.

region
Cornwall

milk
pasteurized cows' milk

style
semi-hard disc, covered with nettles

taste
fresh and lemony

Crottin de Chavignol

France

region
Loire

milk
unpasteurized goats' milk

style
semi-hard to rock hard,
small cylinder

taste
mild to pungent, fruity
and sharp

Crottin is a French joke, or rather it is an Englishman's idea of a French joke. *Crottin* means dung or dropping, which perfectly describes the appearance of this small cylindrical cheese, which accumulates a mass of blue, grey and eventually black moulds on the outside as it matures. Now I ask you, who would refer to something you eat as a dropping?

Crottin de Chavignol is absolutely the best cheese to include on any English cheese board. The French eat their cheese before the dessert, whereas the English tend to serve their cheese board afterwards. This means the English approach their cheese with palates heavily tainted with the cloying sweetness of unspeakably rich puddings. This cries out for extreme measures.

The young Crottin has a naturally wrinkled, creamy white rind and a texture that is soft and slightly grainy with a hint of spice in an otherwise gentle flavour. A cheese this unassuming is unlikely to cut through the remnants of a treacle tart. As it ages, however, the cheese becomes brittle and develops a pronounced acidic fruitiness, which is just perfect for clearing the palate in readiness for the remaining cheeses.

Crottin de Chavignol is made from unpasteurized goats' milk in farms and large creameries and most are sold very young in the UK. If you want the mature ones, you'll need a good cheese shop or a decent cellar and patience.

recipe using Crottin de Chavignol, see page: 112

Danish Blue
Denmark

Danish Blue was probably the first blue cheese I tasted, as it probably is for much of the UK's population. It has always been relatively cheap and readily available. Unfortunately, for many it is also their last taste of any blue cheese, since the distinctly sharp and pronounced saltiness is just too much and puts them off for life.

Early last century, a Danish cheesemaker called Marius Boel began experimenting with several different mould cultures growing on stale bread and eventually added one to a high-fat cheese. Whether it was his intention at the time to create a Danish equivalent of Roquefort is not known but his cheese is frequently compared to its illustrious French neighbour, although few could conceive that they are truly similar.

The Danes are a nation of traders and they have conquered markets around the world with their Danish Blue. Sadly, however, most examples are too young and badly balanced. Blue cheese requires harmony between the metallic finish of the blue and the sweetness of the milk. This is only occasionally achieved. Even in Denmark you find people mixing Danish Blue with butter or cream to soften its harsh nature. If you do buy it, avoid cheese with brownness or over-blueing, a sharp smell or a bitter flavour.

A softer blue is Danish Mycella, which is made using the mould of the same name and more closely resembles a Gorgonzola, although most Italians I know would strongly disagree. The veins are more green than blue and the flavour much milder than most blues.

region
all over Denmark

milk
pasteurized cows' milk

style
cylinder or block, often wrapped in foil

taste
salty and sharp

recipes using Danish Blue, see pages: 129; 203; 204

Doolin
Ireland

Waterford is dairy country and not only home to those makers of exquisite glassware, but also to one of Ireland's largest cheesemakers. Waterford also belies the belief that every good cheese demands the individuality of a farmhouse cheesemaker to impart character to the finished article.

A cursory examination of Doolin's pedigree would lead you to suppose it is little more than a factory-made Gouda look-alike. Indeed, after two month's ripening, the cheese is bland and hardly worth a second thought. Ten months later, however, things are beginning to happen: soft notes of fruit and caramel hint of richer pleasures still to come. After 18 months, or better still two years, the deep yellow paste delivers even deeper, more complex flavours of caramelized butter, nuts and fruit and a lingering finish to savour all day long.

Doolin can be found in one or two supermarkets, as well as good cheese shops, but enquire of its age before buying. If the only reaction is a blank stare back across the counter, ask to taste or better still, take your business to where the owner takes sufficient care in selecting properly aged cheeses and also trains his staff.

region
Waterford

milk
pasteurized cows' milk

style
hard, wheel

taste
caramelized butter, nuts and fruit

Durrus

Ireland

region
West Cork

milk
unpasteurized cows' milk

style
creamy, semi-soft, thick disc

taste
apples, roasted nuts and
damp wood fires

At one time, Jeffa Gill planned to be an organic farmer but she was ahead of her time. She switched to cheesemaking as her only way of adding value to the milk from her cows but such has been her success with Durrus that the role of herdswoman has been exchanged for that of cheesemaker.

For her cheese, Jeffa uses only morning milk, which arrives daily from a neighbouring farm, so she knows its provenance and is comfortable for the time being about resisting the forces of pasteurization. She makes Durrus traditionally in a copper vat and cuts the curd with an old-fashioned cheese harp – an implement not unlike a giant metal comb. This offers more control, particularly when adjusting to seasonal changes in the milk or temperature.

Young cheeses are washed in brine and regularly turned, and the rind develops its characteristic light brown rind, flocked with grey mould. At three weeks, Durrus is creamy, mild and undemanding.

Cheeses leave Jeffa's farm around five weeks old, but I am told some retailers occasionally nurture them for a further four months, particularly those made from autumn milk, which produces the finest cheeses.

It was in Kinsale, south of Cork, in March 1998 that I savoured a Durrus so strong it may well have been one of these. The rich flavours of a long-matured autumn cheese reflected the season of mellow fruitfulness, with apples and roasted nuts and damp wood bonfires all locked in a silky smooth paste. I enjoyed the experience but could also appreciate why my wife didn't.

Edam
The Netherlands

Nancy Eekhof-Stork tells a story in her excellent book *The Great International Cheese Board* about a 1956 expedition to the South Pole, which uncovered a tin of raw milk Edam cheese left by the Scott Expedition in 1912. She reported that the natural protein and fat disintegration had been at work for 44 years and the cheese was sharp, but not spoiled.

The shame about Edam is that is possesses these remarkable keeping qualities yet most is sold and eaten long before its true flavour has had the chance to develop. Many claim it is the perfect cheese for those who dislike cheese.

No farmhouse Edam is made these days, although much is still made from the traditional mixture of whole morning milk and skimmed evening milk to provide a cheese that is lower in fat. It is medium pressed with a thin yellow rind, which is covered in red wax only on cheeses destined for export. The paste is pale and elastic and the flavour is mild with a touch of sweetness, but little else.

The Edam found in British supermarkets is a low-cost commodity cheese hardly worth buying. In Holland, however, those with a black wax coating have been aged longer and are often more interesting. During the 1980s, the Dutch Dairy Board promoted them to good effect in the UK and black Edams were discovered in several good shops – but not recently, however.

region
all over

milk
pasteurized cows' milk

style
semi-hard red waxed balls

taste
mild

recipe using Edam, see page: 150

Emmental
Switzerland

In 1997, we visited a small dairy some 40 km (25 miles) east of Bern to witness the birth of a wheel of Emmental. The cheesemaker's stature owed more to her years of handling one of the largest cheeses in the world than to excessive eating, but she displayed a light feminine touch in preparing the ingredients for her daily cheese.

A wood-burning brazier sunk into the concrete floor heated 1,200 litres (264 gallons) of unpasteurized milk, rennet and starter in a large copper vat. She alone decides the exact moment when the curds are ready to be lifted from the whey, as the vat slowly moves on rollers away from the heat to an overhead pulley system in the corner of the dairy. Fascinated, we watched as the enormous mass of curd was hoisted in a cloth out of the vat and, while dripping whey profusely, was lowered gently into the mould for pressing. The following day, the 80 kg (176 lb) cheese was dry-salted and floated in a brine bath for 48 hours before being left to mature for 4–10 months.

The paste is deep yellow and springy and pitted with regular cherry-sized holes; the flavour is sweet, clean and reminiscent of flowering alpine meadows.

Over the last five years, the Swiss have marketed a longer-matured Emmental, called Reserve, which is worth searching out. At four months, young cheeses are graded and the best are moved to high-humidity maturing chambers for a further six months where they are washed each week to encourage more complex flavours – well worth the extra time and effort, believe me.

region
central Switzerland

milk
unpasteurized cows' milk

style
hard, large wheels with pale
natural rind

taste
sweet, clean and nutty

recipes using Emmental, see pages: 128; 203

Eppoisse de Bourgogne

France

This is a real 'meaty' cheese, which is enjoyed at various stages of maturation, although at its most mature it possesses a pungency that announces its arrival at some distance.

The cheese disappeared during the Second World War and was only resurrected in the mid-1950s. When made traditionally on the farm, it takes almost 30 hours to make and so delicate is the curd, that it must be moulded and salted by hand. The young cheese is turned and washed with a mild brine two or three times a week for four weeks. During the last week, the brine is strengthened with Marc de Bourgogne which helps create a strong-smelling orange rind and a soft, creamy interior.

Until recently, you would rarely find Eppoisse outside France and only then in the very best cheese shops. Recently, one or two British supermarkets have begun stocking it, which is marvellous news for a cheese that deserves a wider audience. The cheese is sold in round boxes and, when choosing an Eppoisse, avoid one that appears too firm or has shrunk. It is perfect when it is on the point of collapse, the outside is sticky and the aroma quite agricultural. The flavour is very different from almost any cheese you'll have tasted – an intriguing combination of milky sweetness and a hard-edged sourness, which is almost overwhelmed by the piquancy of the Marc on the surface. Serve with a glass of Crozes Hermitage or similar.

region
Burgundy

milk
unpasteurized cows' milk

style
soft, small wrinkled cylinder

taste
milky sweetness with a hard-edged sourness

Explorateur
France

region
Isle de France

milk
pasteurized cows' milk

style
soft, snowy-white cylinder

taste
very creamy

This modern French cheese was invented in honour of the US space satellite, *Explorer*, in 1958. Factory-made from pasteurized cows' milk, it was one of the first cheeses now commonly known as triple cream cheeses.

Lashings of cream are added to the milk at the time of coagulation and the result is a stunning 75 per cent fat content and a texture and flavour that is entirely predictable. A soft white rind covers an even whiter paste, which is extraordinarily creamy and almost devoid of any real flavour other than the merest hint of sweet mushroom and buckets of fresh cream.

The one and only Explorateur I have served was purchased from a cheese shop in Surrey in 1989. I didn't care for it greatly but the ladies around the table thought it wonderful. Perhaps I was the only one watching my cholesterol.

Feta
Greece

The poverty of much of Greece's soil is such that only goats and sheep find sufficient to eat. Traditionally, the meat of these animals was real luxury; it was considered better to keep the animals for milk, and the Greek diet has always relied heavily on cheese.

Even today, the Greeks eat more cheese than any other nation, yet their incidence of coronary heart disease is one of the lowest. Probably more than most other populations, the Greeks have discovered the secret of balanced eating.

Until very recently, Greek Feta was still made by shepherds using traditional equipment such as goat skins, and methods such as beating the milk with a freshly cut fig branch. In Greek, *feta* means slice, referring to the slices into which the cheese is cut before they are soaked in brine.

Feta is nowadays made everywhere and tastes of little but salt. The Greeks sometimes add a little goats' or cows' milk but in the main, they prefer the bright smooth cheese that is the result of using milk drawn from sheep that forage the barren hills and plains.

Try and buy it loose floating in brine, and taste it first in case it is too salty. Crumble it into a salad with juicy olives and fat tomatoes, and imagine the Aegean sunshine.

region
all over Greece

milk
unpasteurized and
pasteurized sheep's milk

style
soft, white

taste
salty

recipes using Feta, see pages: 112; 114; 178; 184

Fontina
Italy

I first learned about Fontina from my next door neighbour's son, who married an Italian and settled in northern Italy, close to the Swiss border. This was the early 1970s and, along with flared trousers and tank tops, Swiss fondue was the trendiest way to entertain.

During a weekend spent close to the mountains, his wife introduced me to Italian fondue, known as *fonduta*, made using Fontina, white wine and white truffles. Both the cheese and the truffles were new experiences for me and I have been hooked on both ever since. Sadly, I can afford to eat more Fontina than I can truffles.

Fontina is a mountain cheese, made from unpasteurized cows' milk within the Val d'Aosta. All this and more is controlled by the DOC, Italy's equivalent of AOC. The very best ones are those actually made during the summer, high up in the mountains, where the cattle graze on rich alpine pastures and artisan cheesemakers mature their cheese in chalets or caves or anywhere else they feel is suitable.

Ripening takes around three months, sometimes a little longer, and the texture is tight and dense with just a few holes. The flavour is sweet butternut with honey and a trace of acidity on the finish. Fontal is the commercial version made with pasteurized milk.

region
Valle d'Aosta

milk
unpasteurized cows' milk

style
supple, semi-soft,
thick wheel

taste
sweet butternut with honey
and a trace of acidity

recipe using Fontina, see page: 154

Le Fougeru

France

region
Isle de France

milk
unpasteurized cows' milk

style
soft, thick white disc

taste
earthy

The only version of this cheese I thought truly memorable was tasted as part of a cheese board in a small restaurant in Paris, a short walk from the steps leading down from the Sacré Coeur. Sadly, the restaurant name escapes me but the patron told me he purchased all his cheese from a young *affineur*, Roland Barthelemy, whose shop is on Rue de Grenelle. If you find yourself close to the district, make time for a visit as you will not be disappointed.

Made close to Paris, in the Isle de France, Le Fougeru is a close relative of Brie and resembles a large Coulommiers. The young cheese is wrapped in bracken (*fougère*) or other fern, from which the sweet, rich paste draws hints of dried grass and wood shavings during its five weeks' maturation.

The version I enjoyed was farmhouse made from raw cows' milk and had been brought to perfection in the cool cellars beneath Barthelemy's shop.

Fourme d'Ambert

France

An *affineur* is someone who buys young cheeses from farms or dairies and carefully matures them to perfection. Jacques Hennart is a French *affineur* of considerable talent and in April 1991, his Fourme d'Ambert was judged Supreme Champion at the London International Cheese Competition. This was the first time a foreign cheese had ever won the Supreme title at any British cheese show and since that time, you can find Jacques' cheeses in many good shops around the UK.

With Fourme d'Ambert, it pays to buy a good one, since much of what you find in supermarkets is made in large factories and is acutely dull. Monsieur Hennart's prize-winning specimen stood tall, proud and cylindrical and was made from unpasteurized cows' milk, unlike most of those you find in shops now. The rind was soft to touch and grey in colour, just turning brown.

Inside, the paste was white with pockets of greenish-blue veins, which had developed in the stifling humidity of his own cellars. The mouth feel is soft and creamy, with the flavour of nuts and spice and summer grapes that linger as long as a June evening. I am rather partial to spreading Fourme d'Ambert thickly over a ripe Conference pear and washing it down with a good Sauternes.

region
Auvergne

milk
pasteurized cows' milk

style
semi-soft, blue, tall cylinder

taste
nuts, spice and
summer grapes

Garrotxa

Unlike Britain, Spain has managed to cling to much of its traditional food heritage. As modern hygiene regulations impose tighter controls, much regional artisan cheesemaking is giving way to larger dairies and factories. Nevertheless, DO controls protect the authenticity of traditional Spanish cheeses, so there is little urge to introduce hundreds of modern artisan-made cheeses in the manner of the UK.

Garrotxa is a modern cheese, albeit one that claims descendancy from an ancient recipe. Made from raw goats' milk in the north-east region of Catalonia, it matures for 4–6 weeks into a compact, springy paste inside a natural rind covered with a velvety blue-grey bloom. The flavour is not easy to identify clearly as the cheese undoubtedly demands a love of the goat. Having read several descriptions by different food writers, I feel that no one appears to do it justice. There is a herby creaminess followed by a slightly sharp flavour, but that's as far as one can go. You'll either love it or hate it.

region
Catalonia

milk
pasteurized and unpasteurized goats' milk

style
hard and round with dark, rippled natural rind

taste
slightly sharp with a herby-creaminess

Gjetost
Norway

region
all over

milk
pasteurized goats' and
cows' milk

style
semi-hard fudge-like blocks

taste
sweet

Many centuries ago, in the Gudbrandsdalen Valley in Norway, a young dairy maid had finished making a curd cheese from goats' milk when she gazed upon the meagre whey left in the vat. She heated it slowly until most of the water had evaporated and then added some cream and goats' milk. She poured the mixture into a mould and the result was a brown, sweet, fudge-like cheese, which has become one of the world's strangest cheeses.

Mysost is the name for this type of cheese, which is incredibly popular in its homeland and forms an essential part of almost every Norwegian breakfast. Gjetost is part of the same cheese family and although the Norwegian word *gjet* means goat, the cheese is actually made using a mixture of goats' and cows' milk. Traditionally served in wafer-thin slices if eaten cold, Gjetost is also a popular ingredient in a host of Norwegian traditional recipes, as well as for flavouring sauces and in a sweet fondue.

Norwegians claim that an early version of Gjetost sustained the Vikings as they carved their way across Europe, which probably explains why so few people outside Norway have developed any taste for their unusual concoction.

Double and Single Gloucester

England

Every year, on the Spring Bank Holiday, a group of eccentric locals living close to Coopers Hill near Gloucester race large, round, orange Double Gloucesters down the hill. This tradition stretches back to the 18th century when the cheeses were turned twice a week as they matured on curing room floors rubbed with the leaves from bean and potato plants. This created an extraordinary tough rind, which would help the cheese survive the journey to the bottom of the hill, at which point the locals would cut it up for supper.

In common with most English territorial cheeses, most Double Gloucester is now made in factories a long way from the vales of Gloucester and Berkeley although, almost perversely, several very good examples are made on farms some distance from the county. Mrs Appleby in Shropshire makes a cloth-bound unpasteurized version, which can be very good but tastes slightly saltier and crumbles more than perhaps it should. Butlers from Lancashire and Quickes from south Devon both make a good Double Gloucester.

The genuine article is still made in Gloucester from full-cream evening and morning milk, but in such small quantities that only the best counters will stock it. If you spot a cheese bearing the name of Diana Smart or Charles Martell, then grab it quickly. The same names adorn the only examples of real Single Gloucester, a smaller cheese traditionally made from skimmed evening milk mixed with full-cream morning milk.

region
traditionally Gloucester, but now anywhere

milk
unpasteurized and pasteurized cows' milk

style
hard, orange disc or block

taste
rich, creamy, nutty

Gorgonzola
Italy

Centuries ago, cattle grazed all summer on rich pastures in the Italian Alps and would be herded south for milder winters. One of several resting points en route was the small town of Gorgonzola, where, so legend has it, the herdsmen would pay for their overnight stay with their cheese.

The cows were tired from their long journey. As a consequence, the milk was a poorer quality, which inspired the original name, Stracchino Gorgonzola, from the Lombardy dialect word *stracco* meaning tired. There are several fanciful stories relating how the blueing process was discovered by accident, but in the early days all the cheeses matured in caves in the valley of Valsassina, where the penicillium spores would develop naturally.

As its popularity grew, dedicated maturing houses were built throughout the region and, until the late 19th century, Gorgonzola remained an artisan cheese little known outside Italy. Traditionally, the cheese would always be made from the curd of the evening milk, which had ripened overnight. It was placed into moulds the following morning and covered with the warm fresh curd from the morning milk. Often referred to as the 'two-batch' method, this has now largely been replaced by the single-batch process, which uses the milk from a single milking.

Erborinato and Mountain Gorgonzola are strong and piquant, like the ones your granddad used to enjoy. There are also creamy versions, which include Dolcelatte, not strictly speaking a Gorgonzola (DOC) but very popular.

region
Lombardy

milk
pasteurized cows' milk

style
semi-soft, blue, foil-wrapped cylinder

taste
creamy to strong and piquant

recipes using Gorgonzola, see pages: 158; 186; 204

Gouda
The Netherlands

Gouda has been exported from Holland in vast quantities since the 13th century, and almost every European country, as well as the USA and Australia, now produce cheeses in the same style. Gouda's history reflects much of the history of Dutch trade around the globe. The town itself was one of five principal Dutch trading centres during the 18th century, which attracted merchants from England and Scotland buying and selling cheese.

Some farmhouse versions are still available, although the majority is now made in factories using pasteurized milk. Gouda is richer, larger and more yellowed than Edam and considerably more interesting. When young, Gouda is pale, soft and springy with occasional holes and the flavour is undemanding. During ripening, it undertakes a thrilling metamorphosis as the black rind hardens, the texture becomes very dense and the paste deepens in colour to a dark, creamy yellow.

Goudas aged for 18 months or more are sweet and fruity, with a touch of caramel and a texture as grainy as a good Parmesan. We created a cheese delicatessen at a four-day food exhibition in Birmingham in 1992 and offered visitors tastings of a cracking two-year-old Gouda. Three times we re-ordered stock, but we still sold out by the Saturday.

As recently as 1999, a 14-month-old Gouda scooped the Supreme award at the London International Cheese Competition and stunned several supermarket buyers into stocking it. When Goudas are good, they are very, very good...

region
all over

milk
pasteurized cows' milk

style
hard cylinders in black or yellow wax

taste
mild when young, but rich and mellow when aged

Grevéost
Sweden

Cheesemaking existed in Sweden well over a thousand years ago, albeit on a small scale. The Swedes were larger butter producers and, until the 19th century, they were the principal importer of Dutch cheeses. This is reflected in the style of cheeses they enjoy. Most Swedish cheeses are eaten for breakfast or as part of their renowned smorgasbords, and therefore do not aspire to the complex flavours of cheeses matured over long periods to be enjoyed as part of a cheese board.

Ost is the Swedish word for cheese and is normally included with the name. In the UK, the names are shortened thus Grevéost becomes Grevé, which is arguably one of their finest cheeses. It fits the mould exactly for mild, unassuming breakfast cheeses, and is a commercially produced, milder and moister version of Swiss Emmental. The starter culture used for Grevé differs from Emmental and creates a cheese scattered with the same large characteristic holes but with a slightly softer, creamier texture. At 10 months, it develops the same sweet nuttiness as Emmental but fails to deliver the same long, complex finish.

region
all over

milk
pasteurized cows' milk

style
semi-hard wheels with pale natural rind

taste
faint sweet nuttiness

recipe using Grevé, see page: 174

Gruyère
Switzerland

Gruyère is Emmental's baby brother. It, too, boasts a tradition stretching back to the 12th century when it was first made from summer milk in high pastures above Lake Geneva. The unpasteurized milk from black and white cows bred exclusively in the region is cooked, pressed and matured into a cheese half the size of an Emmental, which at its best ranks in the world's Top 10.

Matured at lower temperatures than Emmental, Gruyère develops smaller holes and is regularly wiped with salt water to encourage a briny sharpness. The paste is dense and gives a fuller, fruitier flavour, which is sweeter and has a hint of nuttiness.

Once described as the cornerstone of European cuisine, Gruyère is one of the world's great cooking cheeses as it rarely strings and is quite the best cheese for topping gratins, for flavouring pastry and sauces and for cheese soufflés. Gruyère has rarely realized its full potential as a table cheese more than in 1992, when an 18-month-old wheel was judged Supreme Champion at the London International Cheese Competition. So determined was the UK importer to win the Championship that he selected a four-month-old Gruyère and meticulously nurtured it to perfection for a further 14 months. It stunned the judges and everyone else fortunate enough to taste it and now, in common with Emmental, the Swiss market Gruyère Reserve, which has been matured a year for a superb flavour.

region
Gruyère

milk
unpasteurized cows' milk

style
hard, large wheels with pale brown rind

taste
sweet, nutty with a deep, complex finish

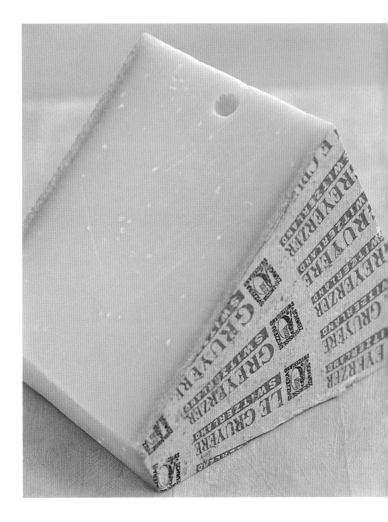

recipes using Gruyère, see pages: 111; 128; 153; 161

Gubbeen
Ireland

This is a semi-soft cheese made in Cork from unpasteurized cows' milk and is somewhat reminiscent of the French cheese Port Salut, but better. Its maker, Giana Ferguson, grew up in a cheesemaking environment, although some distance from Schull in County Cork where she now lives with her farming husband.

She was encouraged into cheesemaking by Veronica Steele (*see* Milleens), but came to it from a suitably qualified direction in that she had studied microbiology at university. The milk she uses is from her own mixed herd, and a labour-intensive process of frequent washing and turning ensures the cheese is meticulously cared for throughout ripening. This cultivates a wrinkled orange rind with a dash of pink and grey. The paste is springy, firm and pale yellow, with occasional small holes.

Gubbeen is normally sold at three weeks, although it can go the distance to three months for an aroma of boiled cabbage and a savoury flavour finishing on a slightly bitter note. Food writer Clarissa Hyman assures me that the name Gubbeen means 'little gob'; I am unsure if she's pulling my leg. They also do a smoked version, which I must confess I haven't tried.

region
County Cork

milk
pasteurized cows' milk

style
semi-soft, washed rind disc

taste
savoury flavour finishing on a slightly bitter note

Haloumi
Greece and Cyprus

Having no wish to upset either nationality, I shall attribute Haloumi to both Greece and Cyprus. Being the cradle of western civilization, Greece probably first created this particular sheep's milk cheese, but over the centuries the cheesemakers of Cyprus have made it part of their culture, too. Everyone else has since caught on and Haloumi has now achieved worldwide acclaim, although mainly made from cows' milk.

It is a creamy white cheese with a rather fibrous, slightly rubbery texture, which lends itself well to frying. Unlike most other cheeses, the exterior hardens while the interior melts in the same way as Mozzarella.

The Cypriots traditionally dip the curd in hot water, then knead it with chopped mint, roll it out and cut it into blocks – a style quite widely available in the UK. It can be used immediately or stored in brine, which makes the cheese rather salty so that it needs washing in water or milk before using. When preparing for cooking always slice, never crumble, Haloumi.

The locals serve it sliced with olive oil and sprinkled with fresh herbs, but I must say this is not to my taste. As an ingredient in a medley of Mediterranean recipes, it is superb.

region
Greece and Cyprus

milk
pasteurized goats' milk

style
soft white block

taste
salty and lactic

recipe using Haloumi, see page: 179

Herrgårdsost
Sweden

Quite literally, the name means 'home cheese' and this was at one time made on almost every farm in the Gotland region of Sweden. It is now made, sold and eaten everywhere in Sweden and is another Swiss-style cheese, but this time the role model is Gruyère. It is a commodity cheese and features on the shopping list of most Swedish households.

Herrgårdsost is a pressed, cooked cheese, softer than Swiss Gruyère but with the same scattering of eyes, or small holes. Mostly it is eaten very young and mild, but a mature version at around 10 months will develop more nuttiness. It is superb as an ingredient in a host of dishes as it melts wonderfully. A very young, surprisingly mild, foil-wrapped Herrgårdsost called Drabant is described by Sandy Carr in her *Pocket Guide to Cheese* as a 'good breakfast cheese for fragile constitutions'.

The principal drawback for Swedish cheese in the UK is the difficulty in obtaining examples matured long enough to develop real flavour. There is one that their marketing people somewhat naively christened 'Swedish Blue', then changed to 'Royal Reserve', which won prizes at cheese shows and delivered what it promised. Mostly, they are suited only to the breakfast table, however, and unfortunately the British don't really eat cheese for breakfast.

region
all over

milk
pasteurized cows' milk

style
semi-hard wheels with pale natural rind

taste
mild

Idiazabal

Spain

region
Basque

milk
unpasteurized sheep's milk

style
hard cylinder with natural rind

taste
sweet, tangy with an underlying smokiness

Many of the shepherds living in the mountainous Basque and Navarre regions of the Sierra del Aralar follow the old tradition of disappearing up to mountain pastures with their sheep in late spring, and not returning until the chill of autumn frosts renders it too uncomfortable to remain. They use the raw milk of the Laxta and Carranzana sheep to make Idiazabal, and the best cheeses are those brought back from the mountains in September.

Sadly, only a few shepherds still make their cheeses in the mountains. Most sell their milk to cheesemakers down in the valleys, where a more hygienic regime is possible, although the techniques laid down by the DO are still followed.

At one time, many of the mountain cheeses were heavily smoked by hanging in the chimneys of the chalets and farmhouses. Nowadays, the tendency is for lighter smoking, just 10 days before the cheese is sold, using freshly cut beech, hawthorn or cherrywood to create an orange-brown rind.

Idiazabal is firm textured with an ivory white paste, which darkens to yellow close to the rind. The taste reveals an underlying sharpness with a sharp tang and the flavour is not immediately of sheep's milk. As the cheese warms and softens in the mouth, the sweetness of the milk begins to assert itself, with the subtle smokiness creating a delightful finish.

Isle of Mull

Scotland

My first encounter with Isle of Mull was in a cheese shop just off Tottenham Court Road in London. I was searching for a good unpasteurized Cheddar to include in a tutored tasting we were conducting close by and the assistant, who knew little about his cheese, claimed to have nothing in stock. On tasting his available Cheddars, the Isle of Mull was unfamiliar, but quite best on offer. Later, it came as no surprise to discover that it was made from unpasteurized milk and that the cheesemakers had learnt their craft in Somerset.

The Reade family emigrated to Scotland with the specific intention of making cheese in northern climes. Their mainly Friesian herd spend up to seven months inside due to the severity of the winters, but this hardly impacts on quality as their feed is so closely controlled. Isle of Mull is made to a Cheddar recipe, but it is Scottish milk, not West Country, so the Reades quite properly refuse to christen it Cheddar. Nevertheless, it can hold its own in comparison with the best from the West.

Pale-coloured, cloth-bound cylinders are matured for up to a year and occasionally develop slight blue veining in from the rind. There is an underlying saltiness from a paste that is just slightly lighter in texture than a conventional West Country Farmhouse Cheddar. It is strong and earthy, with a strange lack of grassy notes, although none the less interesting for that fact. The smaller truckles frequently vary in flavour and there are versions flavoured with herbs.

region
Isle of Mull

milk
unpasteurized cows' milk

style
hard, cloth bound cylinder

taste
strong and earthy

Jarlsberg
Norway

The Norwegians believe their milk is among the purest in the world, putting it down to a combination of the clear waters flowing from the mountains and glaciers through the lush grasslands and a climate influenced by the warm Gulf Stream. The need to store food for long, dark winters fostered cheeses similar to those made in the Alps – hard, cooked and often with holes.

Jarlsberg is a centuries-old cheese, originally made from rich, full-cream cows' milk by farmers living on the west bank of the Oslo Fjord. As cheesemaking centralized into large factories, and farming became more specialized, Jarlsberg disappeared and would have remained lost forever but for the efforts of an agricultural college in Ås, which revived the recipe during the early 1960s.

Jarlsberg is now Norway's most famous cheese export with its red and black waxed rind and bright yellow paste scattered with large holes. While comparisons with Swiss Emmental are inevitable, it undoubtedly possesses a character of its own. It is mild, sweet and nutty, good for a breakfast cheese and easy to use in a host of recipes as it melts evenly. It probably lacks depth of flavour to be a good table cheese, although millions around the world will disagree.

region
all over

milk
unpasteurized cows' milk

style
hard, cloth bound cylinder

taste
strong and earthy

Lancashire
England

In Lancashire, they take their time when it comes to making a proper cheese. Whereas a Cheddar is in the mould and being pressed inside three hours, a decent Lancashire takes three days and more. A traditionally made Lancashire achieves its pale colour and unique crumbliness because it is made using the curd from two or more days' cheesemaking.

In Lancashire, they have changeable weather – more so than the rest of the country. The milk, the temperature and the humidity all change daily, as do the curds from each day's making. When the cheesemaker mixes the curds from three different days, they fuse in a particular way to create a unique three-dimensional texture and flavour, which is the hallmark of a good Lancashire.

If you want to taste the real thing, go to Lancashire because only there will you find a good selection. Kirkhams is made using unpasteurized milk and at six months or more is delicate and crumbly with superb floral notes in a rich buttery paste. Sandhams is made using pasteurized milk from the curd of two days and Carron Lodge sometimes takes five days.

You can find Lancashires in many supermarkets, some of which are described as tasty. Try them if you must, but don't kid yourself you are eating the real thing.

region
traditionally Lancashire, but now anywhere

milk
unpasteurized and pasteurized cows' milk

style
crumbly to firm, tall cylinder

taste
delicate, with superb floral notes, stronger with age

recipes using Lancashire, see pages: 118; 134

Lincolnshire Poacher

England

region
traditionally Lincolnshire but now anywhere

milk
unpasteurized cows' milk

style
hard cylinder

taste
sweet to sharp acidity

Although a recent invention, Lincolnshire Poacher displays none of the unsophistication of so many modern cheese concoctions. This is the only cheese to come from a part of the country hitherto unremarkable for dairy farming, where dry summers combine with easterly winds driving across the lowlands to deny cattle the rich grass needed for large-scale cheesemaking.

The intriguing side to the Poacher is its many guises. Small ones mature quickly for a milky, grassy, front-of-mouth tang, but the larger cheeses develop over 18 months and more into something far more interesting. What cheesemakers, Simon and Jeannette Jones, achieved in the mid-1980s was the development of a cheese that allows the complex earthy flavours in the unpasteurized Lincolnshire milk to shine through in such a stunning fashion and yet still endow an exceptional creamy finish.

My first experience of the Poacher was in June 1996 at the London International Cheese Competition when, up against 42 cheeses from all over Europe, it took the Gold in the 'Best New Farmhouse Cheese' class. A cabinet full of trophies from other cheese competitions has followed. Modern it may be, but with the exception of cutting the curd, the entire cheesemaking operation is conducted by hand. Modern artisan, no less.

Livarot
France

L'Hôtel de la Gare in the Normandy town of Domfront serves a quite exceptional Livarot. A few years back, we spent a long weekend touring the area with our neighbours from Dorset, and our dinner on the Saturday finished with a plate of three cheeses: a Livarot, a Camembert de Normandie and a Pont L'Evêque. All three were superb, but the Livarot was the star turn.

This small, round cheese has the most intense aroma and should be moist and sticky on the outside without any cracks. Contrary to popular opinion, Livarot is rarely at its best smelling of ammonia, although more or less anything associated with a farmyard is acceptable. Around the perimeter are five strips of raffia, there to prevent the cheese from sinking in the middle and which give it the nickname, 'the colonel'.

A good farmhouse Livarot will have been purchased from the maker as a young, white cheese, which is regularly washed, frequently using a tasteless annatto vegetable dye, and matured in humid cellars as it develops a deep orange-brown rind. The paste is pitted with small holes and although creamy, it possesses an unusual meatiness but should never be rubbery. The taste is strong with hints of salt and spice, and is quite gamey.

On finishing our cheese, we asked La Madame where she purchased a cheese in such perfect condition. She beckoned us down a flight of stone steps into a cellar housing several dozen cheeses at various stages of maturity, each patiently waiting its moment of perfection. That's dedication.

region
Normandy

milk
unpasteurized cows' milk

style
semi-soft, washed rind,
small cylinder

taste
strong with hints of salt
and spice

Mahon
Spain

For countless thousands of British tourists, the emergence of the package holiday during the 1960s first introduced them to the Balearic Islands off the north-west coast of Spain. For a country boy from north Dorset, Menorca in 1965 was as sharp a learning curve as you could imagine, and my first encounter with their local cheese was far from encouraging.

The Mahon served in the tourist hotel was young, soft and salty and, let's not beat about the bush, with a touch of acidity that took some getting used to. In fact, most of the British hardly bothered, preferring a traditional English breakfast to this strange cheese.

Mahon is made from pasteurized and unpasteurized cows' milk. Both are permitted under the rules of the DO although one or two local cheesemakers occasionally add a touch of sheep's milk for good measure. Square and unpressed, the cheese is golden yellow when young and fresh, but matures into a deep orange, as a result of washing with oil and paprika. The ivory paste develops tiny holes as it thickens and the aroma intensifies. With a maturity around 10 months, Mahon is quite acidic, with a salty edge and a piquant finish that demands considerable effort to appreciate.

We appreciated it most on a recent visit to Marrakech, where the French chef at the Sheraton Hotel served an appetizer of aged Mahon soaked in the local olive oil with fresh herbs. Somehow, the oil eased the acidity.

region
Menorca

milk
unpasteurized cows' milk

style
round-edge blocks, soft when young but hardening with age

taste
acidic, with a salty edge and a piquant finish

 Spain Manchego

When Miguel Cervantes wrote his epic book *Don Quixote* he damned Manchego forever with the description 'harder than if it had been made out of sand and lime'. That was in 1605 and fortunately, much has improved for Spain's most travelled cheese.

The best is reputed to come from Ciudad Real, Toledo, Albecete and Cuenca, where hardy Manchega sheep have learnt to roam vast distances in search of meagre forage. Summers scorch and winters freeze and the food matches the landscape – rugged and harsh. From such unpromising conditions comes Spain's most 'Quixotic' cheese, one that is often sublime, but regularly infuriates. Know your Manchego before parting with your pesetas.

The proper DO cheeses are made exclusively from the raw milk of the Manchega sheep and will carry the words 'Manchego DO' on the label, along with a little picture of Don Quixote. Beware Queso tipo Manchego: it's a wolf in sheep's clothing; and, while the words '*elaborado con leche puro de oveja*' denote a cheese made with pure ewes' milk, any breed of sheep will do.

As it matures, the rippled rind changes from faint yellow to brownish-beige to greenish-black. Some greenish-black mould on the rind is nothing to fear. The paste is the characteristic ivory white of sheep's milk and the flavour is rounded and rich, but not aggressive. It melts into a balance of nuts and salt and a spiciness that gains confidence with age. The best is expensive, but worth every penny. The Spanish eat it with tapas before a meal, cut into thin triangles, accompanied by a good oaky Rioja.

region
La Mancha

milk
unpasteurized sheep's milk

style
hard and round with natural rind

taste
rich with nuts, salt and a spicy finish

recipes using Manchego, see pages: 124; 170

Mascarpone
Italy

This is perhaps the world's most delicious cream cheese, with a texture rather like clotted cream, but without the crunch and only some of the nutty, slightly cooked taste.

Originally, mascarpone was made with the cream skimmed from the milk used in the making of Parmesan and purists will tell you it is technically not a cheese in the real sense. A culture is added to the cream in much the same way as for making yogurt, and then it is heated and rested until it thickens into an utterly debauched rich, creaminess.

Mascarpone is the principal ingredient in tiramisu, the fashionably popular Italian dessert found in the dairy cabinets of countless supermarkets. Often touted as a traditional Italian dessert, tiramisu was, in fact, created by a home economist no more than 30 years ago.

Any dish including cream in the recipe is enhanced with mascarpone but ensure you buy it as fresh as you can. I always hunt among the tubs in the supermarket to find one furthest away from the 'best before' date – that way, I know it's reasonably young.

Mascarpone also features as part of an indulgent cheese called Torta Gorgonzola or Torta Dolcelatte. Thick layers of mascarpone are alternated with thick layers of soft, creamy blue cheese. I watched my wife first try this cheese in 1988 at the first London International Cheese Competition at Wembley. She was immediately transported to another world. I waited until she finished before telling her how many calories were in each slice!

region
all over Italy

milk
pasteurized cows' milk

style
pure white cream cheese

taste
rich, melting and creamy

recipes using Mascarpone, see pages: 192; 196; 198

Milleens

Ireland

Milleens is as bold as it is idiosyncratic, and as complex as it is variable. It perfectly reflects its maker, Veronica Steele, even to the point that the cheese occasionally varies, perhaps in sympathy with her humour.

Veronica has been a beacon in Irish farmhouse cheesemaking for well over a decade. Her occasional outspokenness in relation to factory cheeses and modern retailing may sometimes serve to detract from these achievements, but she has consistently encouraged, cajoled and browbeaten disillusioned cheesemakers into trying again when once they fail.

Milleens itself is best described as a washed rind cheese in a perpetual state of metamorphosis. The cows' milk was originally unpasteurized, but I understand the switch was made to pasteurization during 1999. In appearance, it resembles several other Irish washed rind cheeses, but as it approaches 10 weeks, the rind develops a confused aroma of fields, farmyard and occasionally even a damp cow shed. The paste moves from firm to runny to virtual liquid and the flavours are a classic case where the whole is greater than the sum total of the individual parts. Food writers and cheese connoisseurs have for years accredited Milleens with a countless medley of flavours – not one is right, but none is wrong either.

I read in Sarah Freeman's excellent book on farmhouse cheeses *The Real Cheese Companion* that Veronica herself described it as 'bold'. That'll do me.

region
West Cork

milk
pasteurized cows' milk

style
semi-soft, washed rind, thick disc

taste
bold

Mimolette /Boule de Lille

France

If you are familiar with the bowls used in crown green bowling, you will have no trouble picturing this cheese. It is round, flat on the sides and, as it ages, the colour darkens from bright orange to brown as a covering of white dust from cheese mites ravages the rind.

In essence, Mimolette is an aged Edam and much argument over the years has failed to establish whether the cheese started life in Holland or northern France. What is almost certain is that the name Boule de Lille was given to a version aged for two years in a cellar in Lille.

The paste is spongy like Edam when the cheese is young, but as the months drift by, it hardens and cracks and darkens. The cheese is young at three months; is called *demi-vieille* ('half old') or *demi-étuvée* at six months, and at two years it's decidedly *très vieille*.

Some French friends of ours who live a short distance from Dunkirk rave about Mimolette almost as much as they enthuse about West Country Farmhouse Cheddar. They sit around the table and carve chunks from an ageing ball of orange-brown, granite-like cheese and drink the local beer. They also grate it into almost anything and once served us curry with grated Mimolette.

region
Flanders

milk
pasteurized cows' milk

style
hard ball with natural rind

taste
sharp and nutty

Morbier
France

At the prestigious Cliveden House on the River Thames in Berkshire, we were served a cheese board one evening by a young French waitress who described Morbier as a cheese from the Jura with a band of blue mould running through it. On being informed it was a layer of ash and not mould, she stiffly declared we were mistaken; she was French and knew her cheeses well.

However, she was wrong, although many traditions attached to the making of this cheese have been replaced by modern factory techniques. Morbier was a winter cheese made using the curd from two days and a layer of ash was laid on top of the first day's curd in order to preserve it. Legend claims that ash was discovered to be a good preservative after a farmer's wife placed a bowl of curd close to the fire to settle overnight and soot fell from the chimney on to the surface. This usefully prevented a rind from forming, which made for a better cheese when mixed with the following day's curd.

These days, the line through Morbier is mostly a dark vegetable dye, such is the obsession with food hygiene standards. Look for a Morbier made using unpasteurized milk – it will be winter made and have more flavour and will likely include the traditional layer of edible ash. At three months, the rind is orange with some light dusty patches and the paste has a springy texture and a grassy nuttiness, not unlike a young Gruyère. Also like Gruyère, Morbier melts with a satisfying even texture, which is wonderful over potatoes or other winter vegetables.

region
Franche-Comté

milk
unpasteurized and pasteurized cows' milk

style
semi-soft wheel

taste
sweet with a grassy nuttiness

Mozzarella
Italy

region
all over Italy

milk
pasteurized cows' and
buffaloes' milk

style
springy, white balls or plaits

taste
delicate, with soft floral
overtones and a hint of
acidity

With one or two exceptions, the only Mozzarella you should allow on your table is
Mozzarella di Bufala, particularly from Campania in southern Italy, either in a ball or better
still, plaited. The cheese is porcelain white and must be swimming in whey or pure water. If
you buy from a cheese counter, insist your Mozzarella is placed in a tub with plenty of
moisture or it will dry out and sour within the hour.

The outer crust is thin and breaks to reveal a soft, elastic texture, which melts as you cut
deeper into the cheese. The centre should be liquid with a faint aroma and an incredibly
delicate flavour and soft floral overtones with just a hint of acidity on the finish.

In the UK, there is a tendency to flavour Mozzarella with olive oil and balsamic vinegar in
the company of juicy plum tomatoes and ripe avocado. Italians, however, eat it very fresh,
on its own with bread, olive oil and wine.

If you buy your Mozzarella in bags, take care to select it as fresh as you can. Too many
manufacturers extract moisture from the cheese in order to achieve a longer shelf life,
which creates a texture more reminiscent of block Mozzarella made for pizzas. Some cows'
milk Mozzarella in bags is fine, but you will need to try different brands.

recipes using Mozzarella, see pages: 119; 133; 140; 146; 151; 152; 165

Munster /Munster Géromé

France

Alsace is home to one of France's most pungent cheeses. Made here, it is called simply Munster, but if produced on the other side of the Vosges mountains in Lorraine, the cheese is known as Munster Géromé. The Vosgiennes cows produce a milk that is rich in cream and high in protein and imbues the cheese with several unique characteristics.

My first experience of Munster was in 1969, at a time when my younger sister lived with her fiancé in the Alsace region of France. On trips back to the UK the two of them frequently exchanged board and lodging with us for a very ripe Munster. At the time, it was a cheese way beyond our experience and one that caused much amusement, as the only place that could contain its pungency was the garage. Their regular visits eventually fostered a familiarity with Munster, which over the years has proved rewarding.

It is a washed rind cheese, which benefits from at least a couple of months' maturation, during which time the rind changes from pale orange-yellow into a rich, wrinkled orange. The smell is anything your imagination wants it to be, but don't let that stop you eating it. Like most properly made washed rind cheeses, Munster is meaty, fruity and complex, but never quite as forceful as the aroma predicts. The locals eat it with cumin seeds. If you can't get cumin, try fennel or caraway, but avoid the version made with the cumin already in the cheese. Also avoid cheeses that have become runny.

region
Alsace

milk
unpasteurized and pasteurized cows' milk

style
semi-soft, washed rind, flat disc

taste
meaty, fruity and complex

recipe using Munster, see page: 188

Ossau Iraty Brebis
France

It is a constant mystery to me why so many people avoid sheep's milk cheeses. They are far more approachable than most washed rind cheeses or even a little pungent goats' crottin, yet so often they are turned down without even a taste.

If you are one of these people, please force yourself to try Ossau Iraty Brebis, just once – you'll love it. It is a mountain cheese from the rugged Basque area on the French side of the Pyrenees, but a quite similar cheese is also made over the border in Spain. The demanding regulations that govern the AOC on these cheeses have played a large part in maintaining the quality. If you see a cheese with the description '*montagne*' you have found the best Ossau Iraty because it has been made using milk from sheep grazing high up on rich summer pastures. A cheese simply called Brebis or Fromage de Brebis is similar, but not made to AOC standards.

The flavour is unmistakably of sheep's milk, but mixed with citrus fruits and white wine. It has a long clean, creamy finish, which always demands that you take another slice. We had lunch one day cooked by TV chef Glynn Christian, who tossed wide slivers of Ossau Iraty and a little extra virgin olive oil into a bowl of filled pasta. With a full-bodied Côtes du Roussillon to drink, it was outstanding.

region
Pyrénées

milk
unpasteurized and pasteurized sheep's milk

style
semi-soft wheel with natural rind

taste
delicate, with citrus fruits and white wine

Oxford Blue

England

Baron Robert Pouget is an irrepressible, highly extroverted, English public-school-educated French aristocrat, who fell into the cheese business by accident. Through no deliberate intention, he found himself the owner of the cheese shop in Oxford's quite remarkable covered market, and numbered among his customers several dining halls in the colleges close by.

The dons in college occasionally mentioned their preference for softer, creamier blue cheeses, more akin to many French blues, and Robert's keen commercial eye was quick to realize the potential of a cheese bearing the name of the world's most famous university.

He spent some time working with a blue cheese creamery in Derbyshire, developing a small, round, foil-wrapped pasteurized cows' milk blue to satisfy the palates of the intelligentsia in the great halls. Oxford Blue finally appeared in 1993 and, at times, it assumes all the characteristics of a noble blue cheese.

Robert visited me a couple of years back and left me an eight-week-old Oxford Blue to nurture. 'Don't eat it until it's 16 weeks', he yelled, as he disappeared down our drive. He was spot on – it was extraordinarily creamy with a host of soft, spicy flavours all in perfect harmony. Unfortunately, it is not easy to find Oxford Blue at this age in many shops – you'll have to visit Oxford yourself.

region
Derbyshire

milk
pasteurized cows' milk

style
semi-hard, blue,
foil-wrapped disc

taste
creamy with a host of soft,
spicy flavours

Paneer
India

In a country of over a billion inhabitants, more than 80 per cent of whom are vegetarian, cheese plays an essential role in Indian cuisine. Paneer is the national cheese and is a staple ingredient in many of the country's light, aromatic vegetable dishes. In the extreme heat of the Indian climate, it is little wonder that the heavily matured and mould-ripened cheeses of Europe have never caught on.

Although Paneer is made commercially and can be found outside India in good supermarkets and specialist Asian stores, fresh Paneer is best. The only sure way to guarantee complete freshness is to make Paneer yourself.

To make 300 g (10 oz) of Paneer, pour 2 litres (3½ pints) of milk into a large, heavy-based pan. Bring to the boil, stirring to prevent scorching. Reduce the heat and, before the foam subsides, drizzle in 50 ml (2 fl oz) of lemon juice. Very gently move the spoon through the milk in one direction. After 10–15 seconds, remove the pan from the heat and continue to agitate the milk gently until large lumps of soft curd form. Cover and set aside for 10 minutes.

Line a colander with three layers of damp muslin and place in a sink. Gently pour the curds and whey into the colander. Gather up the corners of the cloth and twist once or twice. Hold the cheese under a gentle stream of lukewarm water for 5–10 seconds to rinse off the curdling agent. Gently twist the cloth to squeeze out the excess whey.

Bind the cloth around the curds, replace in a colander and rest a heavy object on top of the cheese. Press for 45 minutes–1½ hours. Unwrap the cheese and use immediately or refrigerate for up to four days.

region
everywhere

milk
pasteurized cows' milk

style
white paste

taste
milky and mild

recipe using Paneer, see page: 168

Parmigiano Reggiano /Grana Padano
Italy

Known to many of us simply as 'Parmesan', Parmigiano Reggiano and Grana Padano are from the same family, but from different sides of the Po River. Both are controlled by their individual DOC regulations, but more Grana is produced since it is made all year, whereas Parmigiano is made only from April to November from cows grazing on clover and lucerne.

Italians claim that making Parmigiano is more art than business and few would contest this view. *Caselli*, or small dairies, scattered throughout the region are where the cheesemakers develop their own individual styles, and those who understand Parmigiano buy only from the best *caselli*. Most Parmigiano is good, but the best is a class apart, so it often pays to buy from good Italian delicatessens rather than from supermarkets.

If you get the opportunity to witness the cutting of a complete 40 kg (88 lb) wheel of Parmigiano, grab it with both hands. The bright golden wheels are carefully split horizontally using special leaf-shaped knives and as the two halves separate, you'll be entranced by the intensity of sweet, fruity aromas of milk and grass bursting free after two years of captivity.

Never underestimate Parmigiano for the cheese board. The brittle, graininess of texture is counterbalanced by an intensely rich, creamy flavour finishing with a strong hint of pineapple. It is also the only cheese that freezes well. If you use it only for grating, wrap well and store in the freezer and grate when frozen. The slim slivers of frozen Parmigiano melt the instant they hit hot pasta.

region
Parma, Reggio Emilia, Modena, Bologna and Mantova

milk
unpasteurized cows' milk

style
granite hard, large drums

taste
rich, creamy flavour finishing with a strong hint of pineapple

recipes using Parmesan, see pages: 115; 122; 128; 132; 138; 148; 151; 152; 154; 156; 161; 162; 166; 184; 202; 203

Pecorino
Italy

If you ever wondered how the Roman legions were able to conquer Europe and North Africa, look no further than Pecorino Romano. This extraordinarily hard, cooked-curd cheese lasts forever and enabled them to feed long after their enemies had exhausted supplies. It also meant that Pecorino was probably the first cheese ever to be exported; records show shipments abroad as early as the first century AD.

Like Cheddar, styles of Pecorino have traversed the globe as populations emigrated, although the original is strictly controlled and should always be made of sheep's milk (*pecora* is Italian for ewe). Although once made only around Rome, Pecorino Romano is now more likely to come from Sardinia. It ripens for at least eight months, but the best ones need a year to develop an acrid aroma and a grainy, salty, sharp flavour, which works better as an ingredient than a table cheese. In Rome, you'll often see locals grate Pecorino rather than Parmigiano on their pasta.

Pecorino Sardo is the version produced exclusively in Sardinia. It is soft, crumbly and quite sweet at two months, but over 12 months, it ripens to a cheese very similar to Romano. Pecorino Toscano from Tuscany is far better mannered – creamy and aromatic when young, but acquiring a drier, chalky texture as it ripens. There is a black-rinded Toscano (Nero), which is matured for at least six months and is also much prized for cooking. Toscanos made using mixed milk are called Caciotta.

region
Lazio, Sardinia, Tuscany

milk
unpasteurized and
pasteurized sheep's milk

style
hard drums

taste
grainy, salty, sharp

Pont l'Evêque
France

Third of the triumvirate from the Pays d'Auge, Pont l'Evêque predates Livarot and Camembert by several centuries. AOC versions are made using unpasteurized milk from the same Normandy cows, and the very best examples are found only in the markets and cheese shops of the region.

In the UK, good cheese shops do sell farmhouse versions, but you need to encourage those found in supermarkets before they are ready to eat. You won't be popular, but before buying, open the box and give it a gentle squeeze. If the cheese is rock hard, it has been stored too long at too low a temperature and will never mature. If the cheese gives a little, it will improve with lashings of tender loving care and if by chance it springs back to shape, it's ripe.

Supermarkets store cheese below 5°C (41°F); often their cabinets are close to freezing. My techniques for nurturing cheeses to perfection at home frighten most food safety officers but nevertheless, I intend to share them with you. If it's winter, we store our Pont l'Evêque in the larder or garage. Twenty-four hours before we eat it, it is transferred to the dining room and allowed to develop at room temperature – never near the radiator. In summer, six to eight hours inside is sufficient, but in time, experience tells you the time and temperature needed.

When ready, Pont l'Evêque smells damp and musty, but the creamy texture is light and melting with earthy flavours of nuts and grassy fields. It's a cheese well worth getting to know.

region
Normandy

milk
unpasteurized cows' milk

style
semi-soft, washed rind, small square

taste
light and melting with earthy flavours of nuts and grassy fields

Port Salut

France

region
originally southern Normandy

milk
pasteurized cows' milk

style
springy, washed rind,
flat cylinder

taste
a faint mustiness and a
deep fruitiness

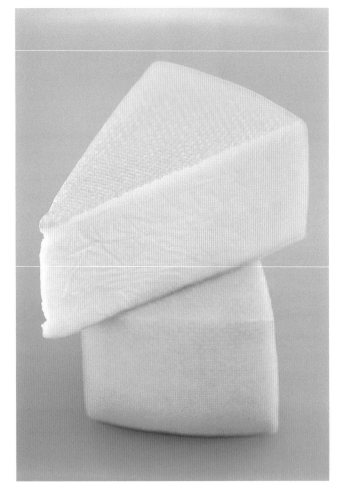

This is a cheese surrounded by confusion, not least because of Port du Salut which is similar, but not the same cheese, and St Paulin, which is almost the same. Port Salut started life as a cheese made by Trappist monks who settled in a monastery in Entrammes in 1815 after learning their cheesemaking in the Swiss Alps. Hence you have a French-style washed rind cheese with the springy consistency of a Gruyère.

Like Gruyère, Port Salut begins life innocuous, bland and buttery, with an elastic texture and flavour more akin to processed cheese. The rind is a pale pinkish-orange and the paste remains creamy white, even as it ages. Port Salut never develops the pungency of other washed rind cheeses, merely a faint mustiness, but it acquires a character and deep fruitiness of flavour, which is not to everyone's taste.

The Trappist monks were so successful that they sold out to big business early last century, since when Port Salut has been produced on a large commercial scale in several regions of France. The unremarkable blandness of most examples sold in the UK is a complete contradiction to its popularity – it is always in demand.

On your travels in France you may occasionally come across Port du Salut/Entrammes, which is still made in a few monasteries around France and is deeper in colour and flavour. St Paulin is another very similar cheese, which turns up regularly in UK stores.

Italy Provolone

Immediately to the left of the Trevi Fountain in Rome is a food store called Il Forno, which I visited several years ago. At one time, this was a tiny bakery, but over a period of 40 years, the owner, his wife and three brothers excavated their own cellar and those belonging to several neighbours as their business grew. Digging was completed under cover of darkness, possibly due to an absence of planning permission, and the soil disposed of in empty flour bags.

Deep underground, you'll now find a honeycomb of cellars filled with rack upon rack of maturing cheeses, Parma hams and countless salamis. The owner spoke no English, but language is rarely a barrier when communicating about good food. That day, I tasted the best Provolone and the best Parma ham on the best bread, ever.

Provolone is Mozzarella's older brother, although you would never guess when looking at the odd mix of balls, sausages and plaits of cheese hanging in Il Forno and very occasionally in proper Italian delicatessens in the UK. Both are *pasta filata*, or stretched curd cheeses, but Mozzarella is eaten young and fresh, whereas Provolone is permitted to age from two months to two years.

The mild, or *dolce*, versions are young and hint of spice, and are better used as an accompaniment in salads or sandwiches. The version made for ageing is made using kids' rennet to coagulate the milk and has enough bite to be used as a condiment and a flavouring cheese.

region
Campania, Apulia and Lombardy

milk
pasteurized cows' milk

style
hardened stretched curd cheese in numerous shapes and sizes

taste
mild to piquant, depending on age

recipe using Provolone, see page: 165

Quark
Germany

The German love affair with Quark is older than time itself, and it accounts today for almost half of their cheese consumption. Hardly a proper cheese in the strict sense, Quark is a fresh, unripened soft curd made from skimmed milk – more like a fromage frais or yogurt.

There are versions that add back quantities of cream or buttermilk or use only full-cream or semi-skimmed milk, but it almost passes without comment that the low-fat version sells in vast quantities.

Quark is one of the few cheeses that is far better produced in large factories than on farms, the mechanics of modern cheesemaking ensuring a much smoother quark every time. Quark made by adding cream after the curd has been gently pressed has an even creamier taste because the rich fat and the skimmed curd remain separate.

Although eaten in staggering quantities by the Germans, Quark has never quite caught on to the same extent throughout the rest of Europe. Cooking with cheese in mainland Europe is integral to the food culture, and Quark really shines in the kitchen – as a creamy base for pasta sauces, in pastry and in soufflés.

region
all over Germany

milk
pasteurized cows' milk

style
creamy texture, sold in tubs

taste
creamy with a slightly sour finish

recipe using Quark, see page: 194

Raclette
Switzerland

This is not so much a cheese as a social occasion, which has gained international popularity through the growth of package ski holidays to the Alps. Raclette is famous as a warming *après ski* dish of melted cheese, small potatoes cooked in their skins, onions and gherkins.

Raclette originates from the Valais region, south-east of Lake Geneva, and is the collective name for several semi-soft cheeses made close to the banks of the Rhône. The round cheese is halved, and as the cut edge melts in front of a fire or electric grill, the soft cheese is literally scraped on to a plate, hence its name, which derives from the French verb *racler*, meaning to scrape.

A good Raclette must melt evenly and should be fruity, but not so assertive that it dominates the other ingredients. Nor must it be chewy; it should be creamy and light. The popularity of the dish has encouraged cheesemakers throughout Switzerland and in south-eastern France to produce Raclette-style cheeses, but the best are still made using the unpasteurized milk from the reddish-brown Eringer cattle native to the Canton of Valais.

Quite recently, we were asked by a British supermarket group to conduct a tutored tasting that included Raclette. It was not popular as an uncooked cheese; most people found it too spongy and lacking real flavour. Incidentally, the best cooked Raclette in London can be found at the St Moritz in Wardour Street.

region
Valais

milk
unpasteurized cows' milk

style
semi-hard cylinders

taste
faintly fruity

recipe using Raclette, see page: 111

Reblochon
France

Any cheese with a good story attached is fascinating talk for the dinner table. A cheese armed with two conflicting stories and a double entendre is certain success.

Reblochon is made in the mountains of Haute-Savoie, using unpasteurized milk of the deep brown Tarantais cattle. The farm-made versions are matured in caves like the tomme cheeses (*see* Tomme de Savoie), and washed to a yellow-orange rind dusted with a white bloomy mould. The cheese is made from a rich, unskimmed milk, which creates a wonderfully smooth, creamy texture with a nutty finish. If you find one in a supermarket, exercise the same principles for bringing to perfection as for Pont l'Evêque.

Now, the cheese of two tales. According to the first story, *reblocher* is a French dialect verb meaning to pinch and, traditionally, Reblochon was always made from the rich creamy milk left in the cows' udders once the main milking was completed and the taxes calculated. Farmers subsequently extracted this rich, creamy residue by pinching the udders quite hard. They were also, in effect, stealing or 'pinching' this milk, hence the double entendre. The other version refers to Reblochon as meaning second milking of the day, from which some say the cheese would often be made.

region
Savoie

milk
unpasteurized cows' milk

style
semi-soft, washed rind, round

taste
smooth and creamy with a nutty finish

recipe using Reblochon, see page: 126

Red Leicester
England

Red Leicester's principal claim to fame is that it makes the perfect Welsh rarebit owing to its exceptional melting characteristics. There is more to this cheese, however, than a mere cooking ingredient although not much more. Unfortunately, it does lack the real depth of other English territorials.

Before the Second World War, the cheese was simply called Leicester, although it had always been made using a healthy dose of the orange colouring, annatto. Wartime restrictions limited all cheese production to a standardized young, soapy commodity and the use of annatto was banned. So began the demise of Leicester.

After the war, very few farms returned to producing Leicester; those that did began using the prefix 'Red' in order to grant it some point of difference. Almost no Red Leicester is allowed to age to anything approaching a decent maturity. A visit to Tuxford and Tebbutt in Melton Mowbray some years ago yielded an example at around eight months, which had a superb nutty sweetness, not unlike a good Swiss Gruyère. Quickes make a Red Leicester down in the Devon countryside and on occasion, these are matured long enough to develop flavour. In the main, however, Red Leicester will continue to pass most of us by.

region
originally Leicester, now all over

milk
pasteurized cows' milk

style
hard, deep orange cylinder

taste
faint lemony bite

recipe using Red Leicester, see page: 143

Ribblesdale Goat

England

Iain Hill is one of those characters who makes life more interesting. He came late to cheesemaking after careers in engineering and retail and, even then, haphazardly fell into cheesemaking around the time that most of us think of retiring.

His wife, Chris, is the cheesemaker and the brains behind Ribblesdale Goat, but the whole business is a family affair with brothers and sons involved to varying degrees. Iain attended a UK Cheese Guild workshop we ran in Sheffield a few years back and quite what he expected to learn from us about cheese that he didn't already know was a mystery.

He arrived complete with a fairly mature version of Ribblesdale Goat, which we added to the 25 or so cheeses we normally feature in our tutored tastings. The pale yellow wax coating hides a pure white cheese with a spongy texture somewhat akin to a young Pecorino. The mouth feel is immediately yielding and almost manages to feel moist and dry at the same time. There is only the slightest hint of goat in the flavour, which is clean, robust and deliciously full of character.

We commented on the difference between this cheese and examples previously bought in supermarkets. Iain replied that if retailers would pay the little extra needed to cover the cost of slightly longer maturity, we could all buy Ribblesdale Goat of this quality in every high street. But they won't and we can't.

region
Yorkshire

milk
pasteurized cows' milk

style
semi-hard to hard wheel

taste
smooth, creamy and spicy

Ricotta
Italy

Most gourmets and good chefs claim Ricotta is the most versatile ingredient cheese, yet it is not actually a cheese. The real thing (the word means 'recooked') is made by heating whey until it flocculates into small white lumps, an original method of preserving the protein left in whey after making other cheeses. This is not casein and so the confusing definition.

The solids are skimmed and traditionally drained in wicker baskets, which accounts for the conical shape of almost all Ricottas. These days, full or skimmed milk is added to the whey to increase yield, which in some ways misses the point. Good Ricotta should be low in fat and sweet as a result of the lactose, or milk sugar. It must have a light, grainy texture and should never be thick or lumpy.

Ricotta is a remarkably useful ingredient in the kitchen. It forms the basis of numerous Italian dishes and has been eagerly adopted by chefs of all nationalities. If you are unconcerned about your weight or cholesterol levels and want to impress, whip good Ricotta with double cream until is has the texture of whipped double cream, then stir in ground almonds or hazelnuts and a touch of sugar. Add either orange-flower water or orange rind and candied peel and chill to stiffen it. Use it instead of cream on anything you fancy and enjoy.

region
all over Italy

milk
pasteurized cows' or sheep's milk

style
granular whey cheese, pure white, usually in a cone

taste
mild

recipes using Ricotta, see pages: 114; 142; 166; 193; 198; 199; 200

Roquefort
France

In August 1992, I visited the caves inside Combalou Mountain beneath the village of Roquefort-sur-Soulzon in Aveyron. Situated at the gateway to the Gorges du Tarn, this is home to Roquefort cheese.

Roquefort is made on nearby farms and dairies from the unpasteurized milk of the Lacaune breed of sheep that graze on the region's sparse pastures. Each young cheese is taken to the limestone caves inside Combalou Mountain where the *Penicillium roquefortii* spores, which create the blue veining, exist naturally. Here the cheeses mature for up to six months or longer. All this is prescribed in the AOC regulations.

Inside the mountain, each cave displays its own personality and imparts a unique characteristic to every cheese. A perfect Roquefort glistens on the outside and, when cut with a warm knife, reveals an ivory white paste pitted with pockets of deep greenish-blue mould.

Initially, the taste is salty and strong, but as the paste melts and touches each taste bud, a rich sweetness of the milk infuses the saltiness in a quite sensational way.

In 1992, as a guest of Société, one of the largest Roquefort producers, I was guided to the heart of the mountain, to a cave as high as a cathedral. There, on an oak table, sat three Roqueforts, each matured in a different cave: Arnals, Baragnaudes and Arlabosse. We tasted them in turn, accompanied by an exquisite Sauternes, and at that moment I was as close to heaven as I care to be while there is still breath in my body.

region
Aveyron

milk
unpasteurized sheep's milk

style
blue, foil-wrapped,
tall cylinder

taste
salty, very creamy and strong

recipes using Roquefort, see pages: 144; 203; 204

Saint Agur

France

A very modern French cheese and one that was most likely the brainchild of marketing people rather than cheesemakers. Some people find the intensity of Roquefort and other similar blue cheeses not quite to their taste, so Bongrain, one of France's largest dairy companies, invented a brand new, soft, creamy-textured blue cheese in 1986 as a milder alternative.

Clever marketing resulted in widespread distribution and the now-familiar octagonal shape and distinctive foil-wrapped cheese finds its way on to even the best cheese boards. Made in the Auvergne region from pasteurized cows' milk, its success has spawned a host of imitators, mainly in the UK, where youth apparently prefers the milder blues. Ladies in particular seem to love this cheese, even those who have spent a lifetime convinced that blue cheeses are not for them.

A word of advice: many supermarkets have taken to removing the foil wrapping before displaying Saint Agur on the cheese counter. Avoid these at all costs because the moist exterior quickly dries out and develops an unpleasant sourness, which ruins the characteristic sweet creaminess and spicy notes of the cheese. They do it through sheer laziness – the foil is difficult to cut with a cheese wire so they would have to resort to using a knife. We always take the manager to task, it's the only way they'll ever learn.

region
Auvergne

milk
pasteurized cows' milk

style
blue, foil-wrapped octagonal cylinder

taste
mild and creamy with a hint of saltiness

Sainte Maure de Touraine

France

This is a 'goaty' unpasteurized goats' milk cheese, which gives credence to the belief that you can 'smell the billy goat' when eating it.

Production is controlled by the AOC, which dictates that the curds must be ladled by hand into the log-shaped moulds and the real thing is immediately recognizable by the length of straw running through the cheese. When young, the Sainte Maure is covered with a downy white rind, which darkens as it matures. The paste starts out soft and grainy, but hardens with age and assumes a much stronger flavour.

In fact, if you find an example sporting a natural dark blue-grey coat, approach with care as the hint of lemon present in younger cheeses will have been replaced by a real goatiness. Sadly, much modern Sainte Maure is made out of season from frozen milk and has a tendency to be over-salty.

It looks great on the cheese board, its shape and the length of straw adding another dimension. Warmed in a salad, it offers something considerably more interesting than a factory-made Chèvre log.

region
Loire

milk
unpasteurized goats' milk

style
semi-soft, log-shaped

taste
strong and goaty

Saint Nectaire

France

region
Auvergne

milk
unpasteurized cows' milk

style
semi-soft, washed rind,
flat disc

taste
earthy, rich and creamy

This disc-shaped AOC cheese from the Auvergne region is made on farms, in small dairies and in factories, so not every cheese bearing the name necessarily pleases.

Those with an oval-shaped green label are made on farms and have been made and matured in the *méthode traditionelle*. The unpasteurized milk is from the Salers cows that graze on the rich grass and wild flowers found on the mountainous slopes. At two to three days, the cheese is taken into special *caves d'affinage* and matured on beds of rye straw. Washing the cheese with brine at around eight and 14 days cultivates a rind mottled with white, grey, orange and yellow moulds. The final maturation is normally undertaken by an *affineur*.

When ripe, the paste is pale golden yellow with tiny holes, and the rind smells of damp rye bread. The cheese is earthy in every sense, with a rich creaminess that sits heavily in the mouth. The flavour remains acceptably salty, but with hints of soil, fresh grass and flinty mountain slopes. Factory-made versions using pasteurized milk rarely reach these heights. From choice, I would drink it with a Château Montrose – that is, if I could afford it!

Shropshire Blue
England

One Sunday afternoon in April 1995, a Shropshire Blue from the Cropwell Bishop creamery was judged Supreme Champion at the London International Cheese Competition. A little-known cheese had come of age.

Despite its name, Shropshire Blue, or Blue Shropshire as it is also called, was developed in Inverness by Stilton-maker Andy Williamson during the 1970s and, for a while, traded under the name of Stuart Blue. The dairy was subsequently closed in the wake of endless rationalization programmes instigated by the Milk Marketing Board and production shifted for a short time to Hankelow in Shropshire. The change of name quickly followed, as did a further move, and all Shropshire Blue is now made in Nottinghamshire, Leicestershire and Derbyshire.

Ian Skailes of Cropwell Bishop began making the cheese around 1990 and gradually, prizes in cheese competitions around the country grew in number, culminating in the above-mentioned Supreme Championship at the London show in 1995. The young upstart had earned its spurs and from that point, most retailers awoke to the new English blue cheese.

Shropshire Blue is a most handsome cheese, the annatto-coloured orange paste in superb contrast with the deep blue veining. Many claim it is merely Stilton by another name, but those who have come to know it well express their preference for its more approachable marriage of the rich and creamy, vivid orange paste with the hint of sharpness in the blue veins. It offers a mellower finish with almost no trace of back bite.

Inevitably, other Stilton creameries have jumped aboard the bandwagon and you will find Shropshire Blue on most cheese counters. Select judiciously, as much of it flatters to deceive. Always taste before you buy and check the consistency of the paste for undue crumbliness. Shropshire Blue continues to please more than most.

region
Leicestershire,
Nottinghamshire
and Derbyshire

milk
pasteurized cows' milk

style
semi-hard, blue, cylinder

taste
rich and creamy with a
mellow finish and a hint of
sharpness in the veins

Stilton (Blue)
England

The Americans love it, the French constantly compare it with Roquefort and the majority of the British eat Blue Stilton only at Christmas. It is one of a handful of British cheeses subject to European controls (PDO) and can be made only in Leicestershire, Nottinghamshire and Derbyshire.

Stilton is also one of the most difficult cheeses to make and mature, as each stage is critical and time consuming. Humidity, temperature and draughts all affect the quality. Young Stiltons are turned daily for almost four weeks, during which time they are cleaned and washed several times. Piercing with stainless steel needles when the cheese achieves the correct acidity encourages the growth of the blue mould, *Penicillium roquefortii*, which ultimately develops an even blue veining throughout the cheese.

The reason Stilton is eaten so much at Christmas in the UK is a seasonal thing. The milk for the best Stilton is drawn from the cow in September; early autumn grass is thinner than in spring and summer, creating a perfect balance of flavour. Also, the weather in September, neither too hot nor too cold, is generally more conducive to making the best Stiltons.

Select Blue Stilton with care – especially at Christmas time. Demand is so great that makers struggle to keep pace and much of what is on sale is too young or, worse still, may have been frozen for long-term storage. The texture must be creamy, not crumbly, which is a sure sign of immaturity or freezing. Always taste before buying as only you know the balance of flavours that suits you best.

Never pour port over your Stilton nor scoop it from the centre. This practice dates back to Victorian times when maggots frequently permeated the rind and outer sections of the cheese. The port quickly drowned the maggots and scooping the centre effectively avoided the bodies. Today's cheeses are considerably safer, so keep the port in the glass and slice your Stilton horizontally.

region
Leicestershire, Nottinghamshire and Derbyshire

milk
pasteurized cows' milk

style
semi-hard, blue, cylinder

taste
creamy with a hint of sharpness in the blue veins

recipes using Stilton, see pages: 110; 129; 190

Taleggio

Italy

Opinions vary as to when it was first created, but undoubtedly a cheese of this type has been made close to Taleggio, near Bergamo, since the beginning of the second millennium.

Farmers around the Alps, whether in Italy, France, Switzerland or Austria, have always herded their cattle up to the high alpine pastures during the summer months. Taleggio, like the original Gorgonzola, was also a *stracchino* cheese, made using milk drawn from cows at the end of summer when the beasts and their milk are tired. Maturation was in naturally formed caves on the steep slopes of the Alps, which attracted a host of interesting bacteria that helped develop a sublime cheese. The DOC now controls the area and methods of production, and most Taleggio is made in factories using pasteurized milk.

Good farmhouse Taleggio is a star on the cheese board. The rind is pinkish-orange with occasional splashes of blue. The rind thickens as it invades the thick ivory paste, which should be lightly springy rather than running. The flavour improves with some ageing. I once left a young Taleggio by mistake in a photographer's studio. Four weeks later, he telephoned to request its removal, expressing some concern about the extent of mould growth on the outside of the cheese. The Taleggio almost followed me home, but what an experience when we ate it! The aroma was of dried fruits, citrus fruits and hay, and the taste was bursting with citrus fruits and roasted nuts. The finish was long and lingering, as the intense creaminess quite literally melted away.

region
Lombardy

milk
pasteurized cows' milk

style
semi-soft, slightly springy, square

taste
citrus fruits and roasted nuts

recipe using Taleggio, see page: 176

Tête de Moine
Switzerland

Three plausible explanations exist to explain how this cheese came to be called 'monk's head'. The first claims Tête de Moine was named after the monks of Bellelay Abbey in the Jura who first made the cheese. Others believe the name originated after the monks passed their skills on to local farmers and subsequently charged a tariff of one cheese for each monk. A third explanation draws on the resemblance between the tonsured head of the monks and the appearance of the cheese after the rind is removed from the top, before the ingenious Swiss device, the *girolle*, is used to shave thin, delicate ruffles.

Tête de Moine is made from unpasteurized spring and summer milk in the districts of Franches Montagnes, Moutier and Courtelary in the Swiss Jura; it is at its best from autumn to spring. The small cylindrical drums are matured for between three and five months to form a greasy rough rind enclosing an ivory to light yellow paste, depending on the time of year the cheese was made.

The ruffles are the ideal way to serve Tête de Moine and feature equally well as a first course served with air-dried meats, in a main-course salad, or sprinkled with pepper and cumin at the end of the meal. The flavour is smooth, firm, spicy and aromatic, with a clean fruity finish when young, but more musty and with a delightful nutty finish when mature.

region
Berne

milk
pasteurized cows' milk

style
small, firm drums with slightly sticky rind

taste
spicy and aromatic, with a clean fruity finish

Ticklemore

region
Totnes, Devon

milk
unpasteurized goats' milk

style
semi-hard, white rugby-ball shape

taste
smooth, mild, yet complex

Over the years, only a handful of cheeses have been capable of convincing sceptics that goats' milk cheeses offer more than the 'smell of the billy goat'. Ticklemore cheese from Robin Congdon and Sarie Cooper of the Ticklemore Cheese Company is one such example, and some would say its greatest asset is an almost total lack of goatiness in flavour.

The secret lies in the way the curds are treated during the making and while Robin Congdon doesn't exactly talk to them, changes in the milk are immediately felt through his hands as the curds are manipulated. Variations in temperature and humidity and the time of year affect the milk, which in turn changes the character of the curds. Artisan cheesemaking is mostly about indiscernible adjustments to compensate for change.

The shape of Ticklemore will prompt your imagination to flourish. The mould used is an ordinary household colander – bright green in colour at the time I visited the dairy – which creates a cheese not dissimilar to a squat rugby ball.

Ideally, buy Ticklemore at three months when tiny holes have developed in the snow-white paste, the texture is smooth and the flavour is mild yet complex. Close your eyes and every wild grass and flower of the Dart Valley is there, with only the merest hint of the goat.

Tilsit(er)
Germany

Anyone travelling through Germany will probably eat Tilsit without realizing. It is the thinly sliced cheese traditionally served with a German breakfast. To the British, a mild, springy and elastic cheese slice alongside the bowl of porridge or cornflakes is hard to swallow, but throughout much of mainland Europe, cheese for breakfast is the way to start the day.

Tilsit began life in the town of the same name, which is now in Lithuania, but in the mid-19th century sat at the heart of the troubles in East Prussia. Dutch immigrants attempted to recreate the Gouda of their homeland; they failed but made an entirely different cheese. The Germans and the Swiss loved it so much they have since adopted Tilsit as their own, but each makes it to a slightly different recipe.

Traditional Tilsit is produced in large wheels, which are washed regularly with brine during the first two months of maturation. These cheeses are subsequently ripened for a further three or four months and can be very fruity with a pleasing spiciness.

Modern versions made in rectangular loaves for easy slicing are sold quite young, are very bland and eaten for breakfast. The moist yellow paste is riddled with tiny holes and there is no real rind as they are foil-wrapped. You will find a slice of Tilsit on all the best German hamburgers, but whether that is a recommendation is open to discussion.

region
all over Germany

milk
pasteurized cows' milk

style
semi-hard, large wheel
or loaf

taste
fruity with a pleasing
spiciness

Tomme de Savoie

France

My first visit to the Savoie region followed a business meeting in Lyon one Friday in February 1974 and, after a nightmare journey leaving the city in the rush hour, a most pleasant weekend ensued. To the uninitiated, which at the time included me, Tomme is the generic word for the small farm-made cheeses of the region; Tomme de Savoie is confusing because almost every cheese from the region is a Tomme, but they differ enormously. The makers frequently add the name of their village to identify the cheese.

I was there at the right time as the best cheeses are made in winter, after the cows have returned from summer grazing on the high slopes. They are made from unpasteurized milk and mature into small, round wheels, which are gnarled and pitted with milk chocolate-brown moulds and smell like fermented grass.

Maturation is at least four weeks, but can stretch to five months for moth-eaten versions, which appear tired and suggest ammonia. Inside, the thinner winter milk gives a lower-fat cheese with soft flavours of mushroom, hazelnut and a touch of citrus.

The evening of my visit, Tommes from every village within a 65 km (40 mile) radius were piled high on the hotel's cheese board. The Haute Côte de Beaune I had ordered was the perfect foil.

region
Savoie

milk
unpasteurized cows' milk

style
semi-soft, natural rind,
flat cylinder

taste
mushroom, hazelnut and a
touch of citrus

Vacherin Mont d'Or

France

Vacherin is as traditional in France at Christmas as Stilton is in the UK. It is an authentic winter cheese, made from September to March, and a rare treat found only in the best cheese shops.

Made from the raw milk of the red and white cattle of the Comté, French Vacherin goes by the name Vacherin du Hauts Doubs or more commonly, Mont d'Or. The Swiss version is made with pasteurized milk.

The cheese is produced in flat cylinders of varying sizes, bound by a band of spruce or fir bark, from which the cheese draws a delicate, resinous aroma as it matures. It is aged in a cool, humid atmosphere from three weeks to three months.

When young, Mont d'Or has a white mould and a mild creamy taste. Later, the crust is pinkish-red and has developed a bold, strong, supple pungency. The paste evolves from clotted cream to a near-liquid texture and at this stage, Mont d'Or is spooned on to fresh bread after first removing the crust in one piece.

Never refrigerate Vacherin; in winter the garage is perfect and do eat it all as soon as it reaches perfection, otherwise the liquid paste will run and run. Serve as a decadent dessert cheese with some warm slices of French bread and drink it with whatever you fancy – after all it is Christmas!

region
Franche-Comté

milk
unpasteurized cows' milk

style
soft, cylinder encircled with bark

taste
mild when young, but acquires a bold pungency with age

Wensleydale

England

I am reliably informed that much of Wensleydale lies within a preservation area where the use of artificial fertilizers and insecticides is tightly controlled. As a result, the grasses and wild flowers that grace these high pastures produce a milk of a particular quality as to be impossible to replicate anywhere else in the UK. It is ludicrous to even consider buying a Wensleydale cheese not made from Wensleydale milk and not made in the dale. Millions do.

Whenever we hold cheese workshops, we include comparative tastings as part of the day. The starkest contrast we offer audiences is the comparison between a mature Hawes Wensleydale at about 14 weeks' maturity and a block of factory cheese bearing the same name. The factory cheese is a dry-textured front-of-mouth sourness, which mercifully disappears as quickly as it came. The Hawes cheese is lighter and crumbles in the mouth to reveal the most delicate combination of honey and soft fruit. There are very few proper Wensleydale cheesemakers left. Do buy their cheese and help them survive.

I could not possibly discuss Wensleydale without encouraging you to seek out and try Blue Wensleydale. Absolute ripeness is needed to truly enjoy this cheese, so taste first before parting with your money. At its best, you are searching for a perfect harmony between the creamy sweet honey of the paste and the steely hint of sharpness in the blue veining.

region
Yorkshire Dales and elsewhere

milk
pasteurized cows' milk

style
semi-hard, crumbly cylinder, small truckle or block

taste
honey and soft fruit

recipes using Wensleydale, see pages: 130; 183

Australian cheeses

For a long time, the only Australian cheese you were likely to see in the UK was Australian aged Cheddar, tucked alongside ranks of block Cheddars in most supermarket cabinets. Of its type, it is not bad, often matured for three years into a drier, more brittle Cheddar than those made in the West Country of England.

Farmhouse cheesemaking in Australia began in earnest during the 1980s, at a time when dramatic changes were taking place in the country's dairy industry. A new generation of farmhouse cheesemakers were inspired by continental European cheeses, as a result of immigrants attempting to recreate the flavours of home. As a result, the range of cheesemaking styles adopted is very wide, with strong influences from Holland, Switzerland, Greece and Italy, as well as France and Britain.

Many of Australia's best artisan cheesemakers are found in the temperate climes of southern New South Wales, Victoria and Tasmania. King Island Brie is produced on a small, isolated island at the stormy entrance to the Bass Strait, where cattle graze on unusually high-quality local grasses, which are said to have grown from remnants of shipwrecked sailors' straw-filled mattresses. (In evolutionary terms, their presence cannot be explained any other way.) King Island's cream and subsequently double cream Brie is particularly esteemed, as is its Camembert, which has an even higher cream content. And the *crème de la crème* is an extravagant triple cream cheese.

Tasmania is also home to Heidi Cheese and Swiss-born Frank Marchand, who produces a traditional Swiss-style Gruyère and a Tilsit at Heidi Farm. His Gruyère exhibits all the full-flavoured nuttiness of its European namesake, whereas his Heidi Barrell is a milder version, more suited to the Australian palate.

Other Swiss-style makers include Haberfields Dairy in New South Wales, where a Swiss and an Austrian cheesemaker work side by side making Raclette, Emmental, Tilsit and an entirely new cheese called Mungabareena. Like a cross between a Gruyère and a Brie, it has a soft texture and its magnificent flavour and aroma are reminiscent of the bush.

Gippsland Blue is a European-style blue matured in foil, made using milk from Friesian cattle grazing on the rich pastures of eastern Victoria. It is made by Tarango River Cheese, which produces several variations of blues in addition to a Brie, and several in a style similar to those made in the French Pyrenees.

Further to the west on the state's dry, flat grasslands is Mount Emu Creek Dairy, which makes a range of sheep's milk cheeses, including Feta and a natural-rinded mature cheese made to a Spanish monk's recipe; the result is a flaky texture with a sweet, nutty flavour. Not far away is Meredith Blue, a crusty-rinded blue, which is superb when made from spring milk and matured for two months. Australia's first herd of milking buffalo is based on the lush meadows surrounding the Victorian town of Camperdown. The Riverina buffalo have been imported from Italy and their milk is being used to make Mozzarella naturally, as well as a sweet semi-hard cheese named Dancing Brolga and a cloth-bound hard cheese.

About an hour from Perth, in the hills of Gidgegannup, Australia's leading goats' cheese producer, Gabrielle Kervella, makes widely esteemed cheeses. Despite their short shelf life, these can be found in shops on the opposite side of the country. In Australia, that's a considerable distance.

New Zealand cheeses

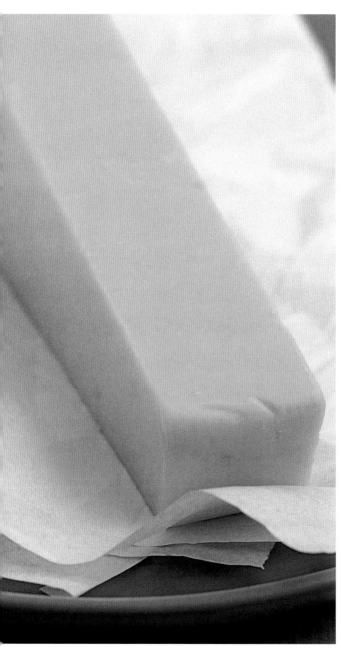

above: New Zealand Vintage White Cheddar

Two or three years ago, a British supermarket chain ran a promotion for cheeses from New Zealand. Several were interesting and full of flavour, most were brand new to the UK and one or two had Maori sounding names that we couldn't pronounce. Sadly, transport costs raised prices beyond the pockets of most people, so you'll probably need a trip to New Zealand to experience them again.

From a British perspective, New Zealand cheese usually means Cheddar. During the Second World War, all cheese made in the UK was a standard, young, Cheddar-style cheese called National. The only cheese available with any flavour was Cheddar shipped from New Zealand, and it's a flavour the British continue to enjoy.

Most is made in creameries, which removes the subtle flavour variations associated with British farmhouse Cheddar but, for all that, Vintage Reserve Cheddar marketed in the UK by New Zealand Milk under the Anchor brand is a cheese of great character. Made only from spring and summer milk and matured for up to three years, it develops a grainy texture with faint specks of white calcium on a deep yellow cheese. The flavour is more salty than most Cheddar, but with a hint of Marmite, and it has a long lingering finish that a Lancastrian once claimed 'made his ears hurt'. He's right, too.

New Zealand's dairy culture may be young, but it is far from restricted to the production of European-style cheeses. If you are visiting, do try Hipi Iti or Kikorangi, two quite recent inventions from Kapiti Cheese, New Zealand's most innovative producer.

USA cheeses

A certain Mrs Pennell, an American author, wrote in 1896 in her irreverently entitled book, *A Guide for the Greedy*: 'Preposterous it would be truly to serve the mild flavoured plebeian species of cheese from America after a carefully ordered dinner'. Port Salut, 'with its suggestions of monastic peace', was her recommendation.

Cheese in the USA has carved itself an unenviable reputation for tasteless blocks, slices and sealed plastic bags of shredded, mass-produced, highly processed uniformity. According to Ed Edelmann, who runs the Ideal Cheese Shop on the east side of New York, most Americans either melt cheese in cooking or eat it as an aperitif, usually accompanied by hard liquor.

Supermarket shelves throughout the United States groan under the weight of bland commodity cheeses and, since the 1950s, American paranoia with unpasteurized milk has all but banned anything remotely connected to proper farmhouse cheesemaking. Thus large factories dominate.

However, a thriving cheese culture has emerged over the last two decades. Farmsteads have taken to developing American cheeses in a more artisan way and the results are

above: Colby; right: Monteray Jack with jalepeños

occasionally stunning. Few US cheeses travel to Europe, mainly because European farming subsidies coupled with import duties push prices beyond the pockets of all but the most passionate cheese lover.

Several arrived in some style in 1993 at the London International Cheese Competition. A smoked Californian Mozzarella, a Californian Golden Colby and a two-year-old Dry Jack cured in olive oil, cocoa and pepper were all entered for the first time and the Dry Jack all but stopped the judges in their tracks.

The Dry Jack was made by Ignazio Vella of the Vella Cheese Company in Sonoma, California; only a single point separated his cheese from a Swiss Sbrinz. The son of Tom Vella, who in 1931 started the Vella Cheese Company with Celso Viviani in an old brewery closed by Prohibition, Ignazio learnt the techniques of oiling, waxing and maturing Dry Jacks from the age of seven. These days, he gives them around nine months, although his entry for the London show had ripened for well over a year.

The cheese is square with rounded edges and it sinks in the centre. The rind has the texture and colour of dark Belgian truffles. The paste is deep yellow, speckled with white and is glass brittle, shattering when cut. It tastes sweet and buttery, with a nutty quality not unlike a good Parmesan, and almost as grainy. When young, a fresh wheel of Monterey

Jack from Vella is soft, rich and unctuous; when left at room temperature for a time, it will spread like butter or Brie. Other examples mix jalapeño, garlic, onion and caraway with young Jack for different flavours.

The son of a neighbour of mine in Dorset settled some years ago on the East Coast close to Washington and, aware of my interest in cheese, returned one year to visit his parents carrying several tins of a cheese called Cougar Gold. Americans happily stuff almost any food in cans if they think it adds to the convenience, but why cheese?

Cougar Gold was developed by the Washington State University in the late 1940s to encourage local cheesemaking and is a Cheddar-style cheese, which the makers claim continues to mature inside the vacuum-sealed tin. The cheese we tasted was almost two years old and was white rather than yellow; the texture resembled the graininess of New Zealand Cheddar. The flavour was smooth, with a hint of sharpness and a good nutty finish and we were hugely impressed. It still escapes me, however, to explain the use of a tin when it is still recommended the cheese be stored under refrigeration.

In July 1978, in a Chinese restaurant close to the exhibition centre at McCormick Place in Chicago, a most cultured English knight encouraged me to finish an excellent Szechwan meal with a plate of American cheese. That evening I discovered Maytag Blue and realized Americans have a blue cheese to seriously rival the best in Europe.

Since the early 1920s the Maytag name has been associated with a nationally known brand of washing machine, but in 1941, the third generation of the family converted their father's hobby of breeding dairy cattle in Iowa into a profitable cheesemaking business.

Realizing the importance of slow, natural ripening for blue cheese, they excavated huge, cool ageing caves in the hill immediately behind their dairy in an attempt to replicate the natural caves originally used to mature the great blue cheeses of Europe. Almost 60 years later, the foil-wrapped cylindrical cows' milk cheeses are still almost entirely hand-made and each one is slowly aged inside the man-made caves for six months – longer than for most European blue cheeses. Unusually, the company has never undertaken any advertising, relying on word of mouth, their own farm shop and an extraordinary volume of mail order business.

The paste is snow white and crumbly and softens after resting at room temperature. Pockets of greenish-blue *Penicillium roquefortii* mould are liberally scattered through the cheese. The aroma is assertive and the paste melts in the mouth to soft cream and reveals a strong nuttiness, a hint of steely sharpness and a creamy citrus finish. The Chinese restaurant served its cheese with dates, the sweetness of which perfectly balanced the Maytag.

recipe using Monterey Jack, see page: 172

recipe section
106–205

broccoli and cheese soup

1 kg (2 lb) broccoli

50 g (2 oz) butter or margarine

1 onion, chopped

1 large potato, peeled and quartered

1.5 litres (2 1/2 pints) vegetable stock

125 ml (4 fl oz) single cream

1 tablespoon lemon juice

1 teaspoon Worcestershire sauce

a few drops of Tabasco sauce, or to taste

125 g (4 oz) mature Cheddar, grated

salt and pepper

sprigs of watercress, to garnish

Serves 6

1. Remove all the tough stems and leaves from the broccoli. Cut off the stalks, peel them and cut them into 2.5 cm (1 inch) pieces. Break the florets into very small pieces and set them aside.

2. Melt the butter or margarine in a large saucepan. Add the onion and broccoli stalks and cook, covered, for 5 minutes over a moderate heat. Stir frequently.

3. Add the reserved broccoli florets, potato and vegetable stock to the pan. Bring the mixture to the boil. Cook, partially covered, for 5 minutes. Using a slotted spoon, remove 6 or more florets for a garnish and set aside. Season the mixture with salt and pepper and continue to cook over a moderate heat for 20 minutes, or until all the vegetables are soft.

4. Using a blender or food processor, purée the mixture in batches until smooth, transferring each successive batch to a clean saucepan. Add the cream, lemon juice, Worcestershire sauce and a few drops of Tabasco to the pan. Simmer for 3–5 minutes. Do not allow to boil or the soup will curdle. Just before serving, stir in the grated cheese and garnish each portion with the reserved florets and sprigs of watercress.

cheese information: Cheddar page 32

cauliflower soup
with stilton

Cauliflower is a versatile vegetable, which can be transformed into a variety of tasty soups.

50 g (2 oz) butter or margarine

1 onion, chopped

1 celery stick, sliced

1 large cauliflower, about 750 g (1¹/₂ lb), cut into small florets

900 ml (1¹/₂ pints) vegetable stock

600 ml (1 pint) milk

1 teaspoon grated nutmeg

1 tablespoon cornflour

250 g (8 oz) Stilton, crumbled

125 ml (4 fl oz) double cream

salt and white pepper

finely chopped parsley, to garnish

Serves 6–8

1. Melt the butter or margarine in a large saucepan and add the onion, celery and cauliflower. Cook, covered, for 5–8 minutes over a moderate heat. Stir frequently. Stir in the vegetable stock with 150 ml (¼ pint) of the milk. Bring the mixture to the boil, then lower the heat and simmer, covered, for 25 minutes.

2. Using a blender or food processor, purée the mixture in batches until smooth, transferring each successive batch to a clean saucepan. Stir in 300 ml (½ pint) of the remaining milk. Add salt and white pepper to taste and stir in the nutmeg.

3. In a small bowl, dissolve the cornflour in the remaining milk, add it to the soup. Stir constantly and bring to the boil. Lower the heat and simmer for 2 minutes.

4. Stir in the Stilton and the double cream. Heat through, stirring all the time, but do not allow the soup to boil. Serve at once in warmed soup bowls or plates. Garnish each portion with a sprinkling of finely chopped parsley.

cheese information: Stilton page 94

cheesy crisps

Serve these savoury bites with drinks or to garnish soups, vegetable dishes and salads. As a variation, add 25 g (1 oz) chopped walnuts, pecans or hazelnuts; season with thyme, black pepper or paprika. When cooled, the crisps can be stored in an airtight container for about 1 week or frozen for several weeks. If they soften, place them in a hot oven for a few minutes to crisp up.

125 g (4 oz) mature Farmhouse Cheddar, Gruyère or Raclette, grated

Serves 6

1. Line several baking sheets with nonstick baking paper. Place 2 mounds of cheese on each sheet, no more than 8 cm (3½ inches) in diameter and at least 10 cm (4 inches) apart as the cheese will spread and form biscuit shapes.

2. Bake in a preheated oven, 220°C (425°F), Gas Mark 7, for 10 minutes, until the cheese bubbles and begins to turn a very pale cream colour. Do not over-cook or the cheese will taste bitter.

3. Allow the crisps to cool slightly, then transfer them to a wire rack using a fish slice, and let them cool completely. Serve or store as required.

cheese information: Cheddar page 32; Gruyère page 57; Raclette page 84

Unwrap warm vine leaves to find delicious oozing goats' cheese, perfumed with Mediterranean herbs and topped with nuts. If Crottins are not available, use chunks of Feta instead and warm in the oven for 5 minutes. Unwrap and serve on rustic bread with an extra drizzle of olive oil.

8 large fresh vine leaves or vine leaves in brine

4 tablespoons white breadcrumbs

1 garlic clove, crushed

6 tablespoons olive oil

6–8 whole hazelnuts or pine nuts

4 small Crottins

1 teaspoon thyme leaves

4 large bay leaves

crusty bread, to serve

Serves 4

1. If using vine leaves in brine, drain and rinse in cold water. Place in a bowl, pour boiling water over the leaves and leave to soak for 20 minutes. This removes excess salt from the brine. Rinse again and drain. If using fresh leaves, make them more pliable by blanching them in boiling water for 30 seconds. Remove and rinse under cold water. Drain well.

2. Lightly toast the breadcrumbs in a dry pan over a medium heat, shaking the pan frequently. Add the crushed garlic and 1 tablespoon of the olive oil and cook for 1–2 minutes, or until the garlic has softened. Remove from the heat.

3. Toast the hazelnuts or pine nuts in another dry, hot pan, shaking the pan frequently. Roughly chop the nuts and stir into the cooling breadcrumbs.

4. Lay 4 vine leaves, vein sides up, and place a cheese on each. Sprinkle the breadcrumb mixture, then the thyme leaves, on top. Wrap each vine leaf around the cheese, followed by a second vine leaf then a bay leaf. Secure with string or a cocktail stick.

5. Place the parcels in an ovenproof dish and drizzle the remaining olive oil over them. Cook on the middle shelf of a preheated oven, 200°C (400°F), Gas Mark 6, for 8–10 minutes, or until the leaves are just beginning to brown. Serve at once with crusty bread.

cheese information: Crottin page 39; Feta page 47

baked crottins

wrapped in vine and bay leaves

broad bean, pear and pecorino crostini

1 Italian sfilatino or small thin French baguette

extra virgin olive oil, for brushing and mixing

250 g (8 oz) shelled fresh broad beans

1 small ripe pear, peeled, cored and finely chopped

drop of balsamic or sherry vinegar

125 g (4 oz) Pecorino, salted Ricotta or Feta, cut into small cubes

salt and pepper

Serves 6

1. Slice the bread into thin rounds, brush them with olive oil and arrange on a baking sheet. Bake in a preheated oven, 190°C (375°F), Gas Mark 5, for about 10 minutes, until golden and crisp.

2. Blanch the beans for 3 minutes in a saucepan of boiling water. Drain and refresh in cold water. Pop the beans out of their skins. Mash them roughly using a fork; moisten with a little olive oil and season well with salt and pepper.

3. Mix the chopped pear with a drop of balsamic or sherry vinegar. Stir in the cubes of cheese.

4. Spread each crostini with a mound of bean purée and top with a spoonful of the pear and cheese mixture. Serve immediately.

cheese information: Feta page 47; Pecorino page 79; Ricotta page 88

griddled bruschetta
with pepper, garlic and parmesan

4 red peppers

1 sprig of rosemary, very finely chopped, plus extra leaves to garnish

125 g (4 oz) Parmesan shavings

olive oil, for mixing and drizzling

4 large slices of country bread or other crusty loaf, thickly cut

2 garlic cloves, peeled and halved

sea salt and pepper

Serves 4

This makes a good starter or could be served as part of a main meal, with griddled fish for example.

1. Heat a griddle pan and griddle all the red peppers, whole, until the skins are charred. Allow to cool slightly, then peel and discard the skin and deseed the peppers. Chop the flesh roughly and place in a bowl. Add the rosemary and half the Parmesan shavings, and season to taste. Mix well with a little olive oil.

2. Toast or griddle the bread on both sides. Rub one side of each slice with the cut garlic cloves and drizzle with olive oil.

3. Place the prepared bruschetta on a baking sheet, spoon the pepper mixture on top and spread evenly. Sprinkle with the remaining Parmesan shavings and place under a preheated grill for a few minutes, or until sizzling.

4. Serve garnished with extra rosemary leaves.

potted cheese

Potted cheese will keep for several weeks in a cool place as long as the butter seal is not broken.

1. Pound the grated cheese, mustard powder, mace, cayenne pepper and butter to a smooth paste, using a food processor or by hand.

2. Add the sherry or wine gradually, mixing each time until it is quite absorbed before adding more.

500 g (1 lb) hard cheese such as Cheddar, grated

3. When the cheese mixture is creamy and smooth, put it into one large pot or several smaller ones, pressing it down firmly to avoid air bubbles.

1 teaspoon mustard powder

4. Pour the melted butter gently over the top. Leave undisturbed until it has set. Serve the potted cheese as you would a pâté with hot toast.

1/2 teaspoon powdered mace

1/4 teaspoon cayenne pepper

175 g (6 oz) butter

150 ml (1/4 pint) sweet sherry or sweet white wine

40–50 g (1½–2 oz) butter, melted

hot toast, to serve

Serves 8–10

cheese information: Cheddar page 32

tarte au fromage

400 g (13 oz) shortcrust pastry, defrosted if frozen

50 g (2 oz) butter

50 g (2 oz) plain flour

300 ml (½ pint) milk, warmed

250 g (8 oz) Lancashire, grated

6 eggs, separated

½ teaspoon salt

½ teaspoon pepper

2 tablespoons snipped chives, plus extra to garnish

1 tablespoon chopped parsley, plus extra to garnish

½ teaspoon Tabasco sauce, or to taste

Serves 4

This hot soufflé cheesecake is a variation of a classic French supper dish. The sauce (Steps 2 and 3 only) may be prepared up to 8 hours in advance – lay a sheet of buttered paper on top to prevent a skin forming and chill until required. Serve the tart with a crisp green salad.

1. Roll out the pastry on a lightly floured surface and use to line a 20 cm (8 inch) loose-bottomed cake tin. Prick the base with a fork and chill for 30 minutes. Bake blind (see page 192) in a preheated oven, 190°C (375°F), Gas Mark 5, for 15 minutes; remove the baking beans and greaseproof paper and bake for a further 5 minutes. Leave to cool.

2. To make the filling, melt the butter in a saucepan. Blend in the flour and cook over a low heat for 2–3 minutes, stirring constantly. Gradually pour in the milk, beating continuously. Draw off the heat and allow to cool slightly.

3. Beat in the grated cheese and the egg yolks, one at a time. Return to a gentle heat and stir until the cheese has melted. Stir in the salt, pepper, chives, parsley and Tabasco.

4. Whisk the egg whites in a large clean bowl until stiff, then gently fold into the filling mixture.

5. Pour the mixture immediately into the cooked pastry case still in its cake tin. Bake in a preheated oven, 200°C (400°F), Gas Mark 6, for 30 minutes, until well risen and golden. Carefully remove the pastry case from the tin. Scatter chopped parsley and chives over the top and serve immediately.

cheese information: Lancashire page 64

aubergine, tomato and
mozzarella stacks

1 aubergine, cut into 8 slices

4 beef tomatoes, skinned and cut into 8 slices

250 g (8 oz) Buffalo Mozzarella, cut into 8 slices

2 tablespoons olive oil

4 teaspoons pesto

salt and pepper

sprigs of mint, to garnish

Serves 4

1. Arrange the aubergine slices on a preheated griddle or under a hot grill and cook until browned on both sides.

2. To prepare the stacks, place four of the aubergine slices on a lightly oiled baking sheet. Put a tomato slice and a Mozzarella slice on each one, then make a second layer of aubergine, tomato and Mozzarella, sprinkling each layer with salt and pepper as you work. Skewer each stack with a cocktail stick through the centre to hold the slices together.

3. Place the stacks in a preheated oven, 190°C (375°F), Gas Mark 5, and cook for 10 minutes.

4. To serve, transfer the stacks to individual serving plates and carefully remove the cocktail sticks. Drizzle each stack with a little olive oil and top with a generous spoonful of pesto. Garnish with mint sprigs and serve warm or at room temperature.

Baked Brie:

25 g (1 oz) fresh breadcrumbs, toasted

1 tablespoon chopped parsley

1 teaspoon chopped thyme

1 tablespoon dried cranberries, finely chopped

4 x 50 g (2 oz) pieces of Brie

1 egg, beaten

Relish:

250 g (8 oz) cranberries, defrosted if frozen

3 tablespoons grated orange rind

5 tablespoons orange juice

1 cm (1/2 inch) piece of fresh root ginger, grated

125 g (4 oz) sugar

To serve:

rocket or assorted lettuce leaves

4 thick slices of French bread, toasted

1 garlic clove, halved lengthways

snipped chives

Serves 4

1. To make the relish, place the cranberries, grated orange rind and juice, ginger and sugar in a blender or food processor and work to a coarse purée. Leave to stand for 1 hour before serving.

2. To make the baked Brie, mix the toasted breadcrumbs with the parsley, thyme and dried cranberries. Dip each piece of Brie into the beaten egg, then coat evenly with the breadcrumb mixture.

3. Place the pieces of coated Brie on a greased baking sheet and bake on the middle shelf of a preheated oven, 220°C (425°F), Gas Mark 7, for 8 minutes. Remove the Brie from the oven and leave to cool briefly.

4. Arrange the rocket or lettuce leaves on 4 plates. Spoon some cranberry relish on each plate and place each piece of warm Brie on a slice of toasted French bread, which has been rubbed with a garlic half and topped with extra cranberry relish. Garnish with chives and serve.

cheese information: Brie page 22

baked brie with cranberries

eggs florentine

Perfect as a first course, light lunch or snack, this is a divine combination of lightly cooked egg and meltingly tender spinach finished with a topping of crème fraîche, Cheddar and Parmesan.

40 g (1½ oz) butter

1 kg (2 lb) fresh spinach, cleaned

2 large tomatoes, diced

freshly grated nutmeg

6 large eggs

150 ml (¼ pint) crème fraîche

50 ml (2 fl oz) double cream

40 g (1½ oz) Cheddar, grated

40 g (1½ oz) Parmesan, freshly grated

salt and pepper

Serves 6

1. Melt half the butter in a large saucepan. Add the fresh spinach with just the water that clings to the rinsed leaves. Cover tightly and sweat until the leaves have wilted, the spinach is tender and any liquid has evaporated. Transfer to a large sieve or colander and squeeze out any liquid that remains. Return to the pan, add the tomatoes and season with nutmeg, salt and pepper.

2. Grease 6 x 175 ml (6 fl oz) gratin dishes with the remaining butter. Divide the spinach among the dishes, making a well in the centre of each for an egg and leaving a 1 cm (½ inch) space between the spinach and the rim of the dish.

3. Break an egg into the centre of each gratin dish and dust with salt and pepper. Mix together the crème fraîche and cream. Spoon evenly over the eggs and sprinkle with the Cheddar and Parmesan.

4. Set the gratin dishes on a heavy baking sheet and bake in a preheated oven, 220°C (425°F), Gas Mark 7, for about 10–12 minutes, until the whites are set but the yolks are still runny.

5. Remove the dishes from the oven and place under a preheated hot grill until the topping is bubbling and the cheese golden brown. Serve immediately.

cheese information: Cheddar page 32; Parmesan 78

manchego
cheese fritters

olive oil, for deep-frying

2 egg whites

125 g (4 oz) mature Manchego,
finely grated

50 g (2 oz) fresh breadcrumbs

about 1 tablespoon finely chopped
herbs, such as parsley, chives
and thyme

paprika

salt and pepper

Serves 4

*Manchego is sometimes referred to as the Spanish
equivalent of Cheddar, but it is more like Parmesan, since
it too is made from ewes' milk.*

1. Fill a deep-fat fryer two-thirds full with olive oil
and heat to 180–190°C (350–375°F), or until a cube of
bread browns in 30 seconds.

2. Meanwhile, whisk the egg whites in a clean bowl
until stiff but not dry. Using a large metal spoon,
lightly fold in the grated cheese, the breadcrumbs
and herbs. Season with salt, pepper and paprika.

3. Form the cheese mixture into small walnut-sized
balls, adding the balls to the hot oil in the deep-fryer
as they are shaped, but do not overcrowd the pan.
Fry for about 3 minutes, until golden.

4. When cooked, transfer the fritters to kitchen
paper to drain. Serve hot.

cheese information: Manchego page 68

cheesy leek
and herb scones

250 g (8 oz) plain flour, plus extra for dusting

1 teaspoon bicarbonate of soda

1 teaspoon cream of tartar

pinch of salt

25 g (1 oz) butter, plus extra to serve

50–75 g (2–3 oz) mature farmhouse Cheddar, grated

2 tablespoons finely chopped leek or snipped chives

1 tablespoon finely chopped parsley

1 teaspoon finely chopped basil or marjoram

pinch of pepper

200 ml (7 fl oz) buttermilk

beaten egg or milk, for glazing

paprika, for dusting

Makes 15

Excellent with savoury dishes such as soups and stews, these are light and puffy and the flavourings can be changed to complement the dish they accompany. Onion or garlic can be used instead of the leek or chives; thyme instead of the basil or marjoram; chilli powder, paprika or cayenne pepper instead of black pepper. Fried and finely chopped bacon also gives very tasty results. If buttermilk is not available, use thin natural yogurt or soured cream.

1. Sift the flour, bicarbonate of soda, cream of tartar and salt into a bowl. Cut the butter into small pieces and rub into the flour until the mixture resembles fine breadcrumbs. Stir in half of the Cheddar, the leek or chives, parsley, basil or marjoram and black pepper.

2. Make a well in the centre and add almost all of the buttermilk, mixing with a wooden spoon or broad-bladed knife to form a soft dough. Take care not to overwork the dough or it will be heavy and tough. Turn on to a lightly floured surface and knead very gently into a round. Pat or roll to about 2–2.5 cm (3/4–1 inch) thick, then cut into scones using a 4.5 cm (1 3/4 inch) pastry cutter.

3. Place the scones a few inches apart on a lightly floured baking sheet and brush with a little beaten egg or milk to glaze. Top with the remaining cheese and a light dusting of paprika.

4. Bake the scones in a preheated oven, 220°C (425°F), Gas Mark 7, for 15–20 minutes, until well risen and light golden in colour. Serve hot or cold, with butter.

caramelized brie
with almonds

A sweet version of this recipe can be made without the pastry. Simply heat the cheese for no more than 6 minutes and drizzle a warm ready-made caramel sauce over the top. Replace the Brie with Reblochon, if preferred.

400 g (13 oz) puff pastry, defrosted if frozen

2 small wheels of Brie or a Camembert-style cheese

1 small egg

1 tablespoon milk

pinch of salt

50 g (2 oz) whole almonds, toasted, to garnish (optional)

To serve:

sprigs of flat leaf parsley

shredded beetroot

Serves 2–4

1. Divide the pastry into 4 and roll out each piece on a lightly floured surface to form a thin round, 5 cm (2 inches) larger than the cheeses.

2. Make an egg glaze by beating together the egg, milk and salt in a small bowl. Place each cheese wheel in the middle of a pastry round. Brush the pastry around the cheese with a little of the egg glaze and then top each with a second pastry round. Press all around the edges of the pastry rounds to seal the pieces together well, then trim the pastry to give a 2.5 cm (1 inch) border.

3. Transfer the 2 pastry-covered cheeses to a baking sheet and leave to chill for 30 minutes. Brush the tops and sides with more of the egg glaze and score the tops with a sharp knife to form a pattern. Cut 2 small slits in each top to allow steam to escape.

4. Bake in a preheated oven, 220°C (425°F), Gas Mark 7, for 20 minutes, until the pastry is puffed up and golden. Allow to stand for 10 minutes before garnishing with toasted almonds, if using, and serving with flat leaf parsley and shredded beetroot.

cheese information: Brie page 22; Camembert page 27; Reblochon page 85

three-cheese
fondue

1 garlic clove, halved

50 g (2 oz) butter

1–2 celery sticks, finely chopped

300 ml (½ pint) dry white wine

375 g (12 oz) Emmental, grated

375 g (12 oz) Gruyère, grated

75 g (3 oz) Parmesan, freshly grated

pinch of mustard powder

pinch of ground nutmeg

pinch of cayenne pepper

3 teaspoons cornflour

2 tablespoons brandy

To serve:

cooked peeled king prawns

cubes of brown or French bread

Serves 4

1. Rub the inside of a fondue pot with the cut clove of garlic, then discard the garlic. Add the butter to the pot and heat over a medium heat on the stove until it melts. Add the celery and fry for 5–10 minutes. Stir in the wine and heat gently.

2. Gradually add the 3 cheeses, stirring until melted. Season with the mustard powder, nutmeg and cayenne pepper.

3. Blend the cornflour in a cup with the brandy then add to the fondue. Bring to the boil and cook for 10 minutes, stirring constantly.

4. Transfer the fondue pot to the table and keep warm over a burner. Serve with king prawns and cubes of bread to dip into the fondue.

cheese information: Emmental page 44; Gruyère page 57; Parmesan page 78

stilton and chive fondue

1 garlic clove, halved

1 tablespoon cornflour

150 ml (¼ pint) white wine

250 g (8 oz) Stilton or Danish Blue, crumbled

300 ml (½ pint) soured cream

1 tablespoon chopped parsley

3 tablespoons snipped chives

salt and pepper

To serve:

12 red-skinned new potatoes, boiled and halved

250 g (8 oz) broccoli florets

250 g (8 oz) cauliflower florets

Serves 4–6

1. Rub the inside of an earthenware fondue pot with the cut clove of garlic, then discard the garlic.

2. Blend the cornflour in a cup with a little of the wine. Add the remaining wine to the fondue pot, and bring to the boil. Add the cornflour mixture and cook, stirring constantly, until thickened.

3. Add the crumbled cheese and stir until melted, then add the soured cream, parsley, chives and salt and pepper to taste.

4. Transfer the fondue pot to the table and keep warm over a burner. Serve with cooked new potatoes and raw broccoli and cauliflower florets to dip into the fondue.

cheese information: Danish Blue page 40; Stilton page 94

spiced pears with blue wensleydale

8 small conference or comice pears

½ lemon, plus strips of peel

4 whole cloves

1 star anise

1 cinnamon stick

2 tablespoons caster sugar

½ tablespoon black peppercorns

2 teaspoons mustard seeds

600 ml (1 pint) red wine

To serve:

250 g (8 oz) Blue Wensleydale or Harbourne Blue, cut into thick slices or wedges

mixed salad leaves, such as rocket, mustard and baby Swiss chard

Scottish oatcakes

Serves 8

The assertive flavour of this English blue cheese marries well with the punchy flavours of pears steeped overnight in mulled wine. This makes a wonderful winter evening supper with pickles and chutneys or a light and breezy summer time salad.

1. Thinly peel the pears and rub them all over with the halved lemon to prevent the pear flesh from discolouring.

2. In a medium sized saucepan, just large enough to stand all the pears upright, place the cloves, star anise, cinnamon, sugar, peppercorns and mustard seeds. Pour in the red wine and simmer gently for 10 minutes. Add the pears to the wine and simmer for 10 minutes. Remove from the heat.

3. Allow the pears to cool in the spiced wine, then refrigerate overnight in the wine.

4. Remove the pears from the red wine marinade and serve with thick slices or wedges of Blue Wensleydale or Harbourne Blue cheese, assorted salad leaves and a pile of oatcakes.

cheese information: Blue Wensleydale page 101; Harbourne Blue page 19

sole with **parmesan** and marsala

flour, for dusting

4 Dover or lemon sole, skinned

75 g (3 oz) butter

25 g (1 oz) Parmesan, freshly grated, plus extra to serve

50 ml (2 fl oz) fish stock

3 tablespoons Marsala or dry white wine

salt and pepper

To garnish:

sprigs of flat leaf parsley

lemon wedges

Serves 4

The cheese and wine in this recipe make a rich, luxurious sauce for the fish. Ideally, Dover sole should be used, since it is the finest quality. Lemon sole makes a perfectly good substitute, but it does have a different flavour.

1. Place a little flour in a shallow bowl and season with salt and pepper. Dip the sole in the seasoned flour to dust them lightly on both sides. Shake off any excess flour.

2. Heat the butter in a large frying pan. Add the floured sole and cook over a gentle heat until they are golden brown on both sides, turning them once.

3. Sprinkle the grated Parmesan over the sole and then cook very gently for another 2–3 minutes, until the cheese melts.

4. Add the fish stock and the Marsala or dry white wine. Cover the pan and cook over a very low heat for 4–5 minutes, until the sole are cooked and tender and the sauce reduced.

5. Serve the sole sprinkled with extra grated Parmesan and garnished with sprigs of flat leaf parsley and lemon wedges.

cheese information: Parmesan page 78

baked cod with mozzarella and tomato sauce

You could use any firm-fleshed white fish for this dish. Haddock is a good, everyday substitute for cod. For an exotic touch you could try shark steaks, and for a special occasion use halibut. Serve with a tomato and fresh basil salad and fresh bread, if liked.

400 g (13 oz) can chopped tomatoes

1 garlic clove, crushed

2 tablespoons olive oil, plus extra for brushing

1 teaspoon chopped thyme

1 teaspoon grated lemon rind

pinch of sugar

2 tablespoons chopped basil, plus extra sprigs to garnish

4 x 175 g (6 oz) cod steaks, washed and dried

50 g (2 oz) pitted black olives

250 g (8 oz) Mozzarella, thinly sliced

salt and pepper

Serves 4

1. Place the canned tomatoes, crushed garlic, olive oil, thyme, lemon rind, sugar and a little seasoning in a small saucepan. Bring to the boil over a low heat, cover and simmer for 30 minutes. Remove the lid and cook for a further 15 minutes, until the sauce is thick. Stir in the basil and set aside to cool.

2. Place the cod steaks in a shallow, oiled ovenproof dish. Pour over the tomato sauce and scatter over the olives. Finally, place the slices of Mozzarella over the fish to cover them completely.

3. Cover the dish loosely with foil and bake in a preheated oven, 200°C (400°F), Gas Mark 6, for 20 minutes. Remove the foil and bake for a further 10–15 minutes, until the cheese is bubbling and golden and the fish is cooked through. Garnish with extra basil sprigs and serve immediately.

plaice with applewood and parsley crust

4 x 150 g (5 oz) plaice fillets

75 g (3 oz) dry white breadcrumbs

3 tablespoons chopped
flat leaf parsley

1 garlic clove, crushed

finely grated rind of ½ lemon

25 g (1 oz) walnuts, finely chopped

25 g (1 oz) Applewood or
Lancashire, finely grated

2 tablespoons seasoned flour

1 egg, beaten

25 g (1 oz) butter

1 tablespoon olive oil

salt and pepper

To serve:

lemon wedges

25 g (1 oz) butter, melted

sprigs of dill

Serves 4

The dry, smoky flavour of Applewood works well in this rich green crust – a modern British interpretation of gremolata. Make it good and rustic and adhere it thickly to the tender fillets of plaice. If you prefer, cod or haddock would work equally well. Serve with French fries and sweet mustard sauce or with plenty of mixed green vegetables.

1. Season the plaice fillets on both sides with salt and pepper.

2. Place half the breadcrumbs in a blender or food processor with the chopped parsley and garlic and blend together until the breadcrumbs are slightly green. Mix these breadcrumbs into the remaining crumbs, together with the grated lemon rind, chopped walnuts and grated cheese. Season with salt and pepper and mix together well.

3. Sprinkle a little seasoned flour over each plaice fillet, then dip the flesh side of each fillet into the beaten egg. Place the fillets, skin side down, on preheated baking sheets and sprinkle the breadcrumb mixture over the fish.

4. Melt the butter with the olive oil and drizzle over the fish. Cook on the top shelf of a preheated oven, 200°C (400°F), Gas Mark 6, for 10–12 minutes, or until the crust is golden brown and the fish cooked through. Serve with wedges of lemon, a drizzle of melted butter and sprigs of dill.

cheese information: Applewood page 15; Lancashire page 64

layered fish pie
with cheddar

500 g (1 lb) firm white fish fillets, such as cod or haddock, rinsed

1 bay leaf

6 white peppercorns

1.2 litres (2 pints) milk

2 tablespoons olive oil

2 large onions, thinly sliced

500 g (1 lb) potatoes, thinly sliced

2 garlic cloves

ground nutmeg

500 g (1 lb) tomatoes, skinned and thinly sliced

½ teaspoon dried dill

4 large hard-boiled eggs, shelled and sliced

2 large eggs, beaten

50 g (2 oz) Cheddar, grated

salt and pepper

sprigs of dill, to garnish

Serves 6

1. Place the fish in a shallow pan with the bay leaf, peppercorns and half of the milk. Bring to the boil and simmer gently, covered, for 15 minutes, or until the fish flakes easily.

2. Meanwhile, in another pan, heat the oil, add the onions and fry gently for 15 minutes, until soft and golden. Remove with a slotted spoon and set aside.

3. Layer the potato slices in another saucepan, sprinkling each layer with slivers of garlic from one of the cloves, nutmeg, salt and pepper. Cover with the remaining milk, bring to the boil, then simmer gently for about 8–10 minutes, until just cooked.

4. Rub a casserole with the remaining garlic clove and reserve it. Spoon the fried onions into the casserole. Place the fish on top, straining and reserving the milk from the fish pan.

5. Add the tomatoes to the oil left in the onion pan. Stir-fry over a high heat for 2–3 minutes, until they begin to soften and exude liquid. Lay the tomatoes on top of the fish and sprinkle with dried dill. Bury the reserved garlic clove in the mixture.

6. Drain the potatoes, reserving the milk. Arrange the hard-boiled egg slices over the tomatoes, then cover with the potatoes.

7. Whisk the beaten eggs into the reserved milk. Pour over the fish, adding a little extra milk if necessary, so that the liquid is level with the potatoes. Sprinkle the cheese on top. Cook in a preheated oven, 180°C (350°F), Gas Mark 4, for 12–20, minutes until the 'custard' is very lightly set (you don't want it too solid or the pie will be dry). Garnish with sprigs of dill and serve immediately.

cheese information: Cheddar page 32

chicken stuffed
with bel paese and parma ham

1. Place each chicken breast between 2 sheets of greaseproof paper and hammer with a rolling pin until thin. Season lightly with salt and pepper.

2. Place a slice of Parma ham on top of each chicken breast, then a slice of Bel Paese and finally an asparagus spear. Roll up each breast and wind a length of cotton thread around to hold it. Tie securely and dust with flour.

3. Heat 25 g (1 oz) of the butter with the oil in a frying pan. Sauté the chicken rolls over a very low heat, turning them frequently, for about 15 minutes, or until tender, cooked and golden. Remove the lengths of cotton and transfer the rolls to a serving dish and keep warm.

4. Add the Marsala or wine, chicken stock and the remaining butter to the juices in the frying pan. Bring to the boil and simmer for 3–4 minutes, scraping the base of the pan with a wooden spoon to pick up all the sediment off the bottom. Spoon the sauce over the chicken, garnish with parsley sprigs and serve with extra asparagus spears, if liked.

4 boneless, skinless chicken breasts

4 thin small slices of Parma ham

4 thin slices of Bel Paese

4 cooked or canned asparagus spears, plus extra to serve

flour, for dusting

50 g (2 oz) butter

1 tablespoon olive oil

6 tablespoons Marsala or dry white wine

2 tablespoons chicken stock

salt and pepper

sprigs of flat leaf parsley, to garnish

Serves 4

2 tablespoons oil

1 small onion, finely chopped

175 g (6 oz) boneless, skinless
chicken, minced

200 g (7 oz) artichoke hearts in olive
oil, drained and chopped

65 g (2½ oz) full-fat soft cheese

handful of basil leaves, chopped,
plus extra to garnish

8 ready-to-cook cannelloni tubes

3 tablespoons grated Parmesan

salt and pepper

Tomato Sauce:

1 tablespoon olive oil

1 large onion, finely chopped

2 garlic cloves, crushed

400 g (13 oz) can chopped tomatoes

2 teaspoons sugar

3 tablespoons tomato purée

150 ml (¼ pint) water or
chicken stock

1 teaspoon dried mixed herbs

Serves 4

1. First prepare the tomato sauce. Heat the oil in a pan. Add the onion and garlic and cook over a moderate heat until soft but not brown. Add the remaining ingredients. Bring to the boil, stirring occasionally. Lower the heat, cover and simmer for 40 minutes.

2. To make the filling, heat the oil in a frying pan. Add the onion and fry over a moderate heat until soft but not brown. Add the minced chicken and cook for a few minutes, until just cooked. Remove from the heat. Stir in the artichoke hearts, soft cheese and basil, with salt and pepper to taste. Mix well and use to fill the cannelloni tubes.

3. Place the filled cannelloni in a lightly greased ovenproof dish. Pour over the prepared tomato sauce and sprinkle with the grated Parmesan. Bake on the middle shelf of a preheated oven, 190°C (375°F), Gas Mark 5, for 40 minutes. Serve immediately, garnished with extra basil leaves.

cheese information: Parmesan page 78

chicken and
artichoke cannelloni

chicken with mozzarella
and sun-dried tomatoes

4 boneless, skinless chicken breasts

125 g (4 oz) Mozzarella, cut
into 4 thick slices

4 large pieces of sun-dried tomato
in oil, drained

2 tablespoons olive oil

8 slices of Parma ham

pepper

lemon wedges, to serve (optional)

Serves 4

*These tasty stuffed chicken breasts are delicious served
with roasted vine tomatoes and rocket leaves, drizzled
with a little olive oil.*

1. Cut a long horizontal slit through the thickest part
of each chicken breast without cutting right through.

2. Stuff each chicken breast with a thick slice of
Mozzarella and a large piece of sun-dried tomato.
Season with pepper.

3. Heat the oil in a shallow flameproof casserole,
add the stuffed chicken breasts and sauté for
4 minutes on each side. Transfer the casserole to a
preheated oven, 200°C (400°F), Gas Mark 6, and
cook for 15 minutes. While the chicken is cooking,
pan-fry the Parma ham for 1 minute only, just to
make it crispy.

4. Place the cooked chicken on serving plates, and
top each with 2 slices of the Parma ham. Serve each
with a wedge of lemon, if liked.

cheese information: Mozzarella page 73

chicken stuffed
with spinach and ricotta

4 boneless, skinless chicken breasts

125 g (4 oz) Ricotta, crumbled

125 g (4 oz) cooked spinach,
squeezed dry and chopped

¼ teaspoon grated nutmeg

8 slices of Parma ham

2 tablespoons olive oil

salt and pepper

Serves 4

1. Cut a long horizontal slit through the thickest part of each chicken breast without cutting right through.

2. Place the Ricotta in a bowl. Add the chopped spinach with the grated nutmeg. Season with salt and pepper and mix well.

3. Divide the stuffing between the 4 chicken breasts. Wrap each one in 2 pieces of Parma ham, wrapping the ham around the chicken to totally enclose the meat.

4. Heat the oil in a shallow flameproof casserole, add the chicken breasts and sauté for 4 minutes on each side, or until the ham starts to brown. Transfer the casserole to a preheated oven, 200°C (400°F), Gas Mark 6, and cook for 15 minutes. The ham should be browned and slightly crunchy on the outside and the chicken moist and soft.

cheese information: Ricotta page 88

beef braised with beer
and cheddar dumplings

2 tablespoons vegetable oil

2 onions, sliced

750 g (1½ lb) stewing beef, cubed

1 rounded tablespoon plain flour

1 teaspoon brown sugar

pinch of cinnamon

300 ml (½ pint) brown ale

salt and pepper

Dumplings:

125 g (4 oz) self-raising flour

50 g (2 oz) shredded suet or melted margarine

25 g (1 oz) Cheddar or Red Leicester, grated

2–3 tablespoons water

Serves 4

1. Heat the oil in a large saucepan and cook the onions until soft. Transfer the onions to a casserole.

2. Add the cubes of beef to the saucepan and quickly brown on all sides. Then add the flour and let it cook for 1 minute, stirring from time to time.

3. Add the sugar and cinnamon, then gradually pour in the beer. Stir well and add salt and pepper to taste.

4. Transfer the meat and gravy to the casserole. Cover and cook in a preheated oven, 180°C (350°F), Gas Mark 4, for 30 minutes, then reduce the oven temperature to 160°C (325°F), Gas Mark 3, and continue cooking for a further 1 hour.

5. Meanwhile, to make the dumplings, mix together all the dry ingredients in a bowl. Add the water gradually, adding a little more if needed to make a fairly slack dough.

6. Using floured hands, break the dough into 8 small pieces, then roll into little balls with your palms. Chill until required.

7. After 1½ hours' cooking time, test the meat with a fork. If necessary, cook for a further 30 minutes. If the casserole seems dry, add a little water, or more brown ale.

8. About 20 minutes before the meat will be ready, place the dumplings on top of the casserole. Leave off the lid and cook until they are risen – about 20–30 minutes.

cheese information: Cheddar page 32; Red Leicester page 86

1 tablespoon crushed
black peppercorns

1 teaspoon crushed chilli
flakes (optional)

4 x 175 g (6 oz) rump steaks,
at least 2.5 cm (1 inch) thick

3 tablespoons vegetable oil

2 tablespoons creamed horseradish

175 g (6 oz) Roquefort, crumbled

½ tablespoon chopped flat leaf
parsley, plus extra to garnish

Serves 4

A traditional mix – the king of European blue cheeses, beef steak and horseradish. Serve with fried sweet potatoes and a cooked beetroot purée made with chives and a generous spoonful of cream, or with a crisp mix of salad leaves. However, the best way has to be with the steak sandwiched, while still piping hot, within the best baguette you can find.

1. Mix together the crushed black peppercorns and the chilli flakes, if using, and place on a plate. Press one side of each steak into the mixture to create a light crust.

2. Heat the oil in a large frying pan until very hot and then add the steaks, crust downwards. Sear on both sides until golden brown. Turn the steaks peppercorn crust upwards.

3. Mix the creamed horseradish and crumbled Roquefort together with the chopped parsley and spoon on to the top of each steak.

4. Cook the steaks for 2 further minutes for medium; 4–5 minutes for well-done meat. Then place briefly under a preheated hot grill to slightly brown the Roquefort crust. Serve immediately, garnished with extra flat leaf parsley.

cheese information: Roquefort page 89

fillet steak
with roquefort and horseradish

beef steaks with mozzarella

2 tablespoons vegetable oil

4 beef steaks

2 tablespoons olive oil

1 onion, finely chopped

1 garlic clove, crushed

1 courgette, diced

1 yellow pepper, cored, deseeded and diced

1 aubergine, diced

6 plum tomatoes, skinned and diced

10 basil leaves, chopped

4 thick slices of Mozzarella

salt and pepper

sprigs of basil or flat leaf parsley, to garnish

Serves 4

1. Heat the vegetable oil in a shallow pan over a medium heat. Add the steaks and cook for about 2–4 minutes on each side, or according to taste. Season, remove from the pan and keep warm.

2. Add the olive oil to the same pan and sauté the onion and garlic until golden and crispy. Add the courgette, yellow pepper and aubergine, and cook for a few minutes. Add the tomatoes to the pan with a little salt and pepper, then add the chopped basil.

3. Place the steaks on a baking sheet. Top each one with a quarter of the vegetables and a thick slice of Mozzarella. Place in a preheated oven, 200°C (400°F), Gas Mark 6, for about 5 minutes, or until the Mozzarella is slightly melted. Serve garnished with a sprig of basil or parsley.

parmesan-breaded
lamb chops

1. Season the flour with salt and pepper and the sesame seeds. Dip the lamb into the seasoned flour, coating it evenly all over. Mix together the grated Parmesan and breadcrumbs and season with salt and pepper.

75 g (3 oz) plain flour

1 tablespoon sesame seeds

2. Dip the lamb first in the beaten egg and then in the Parmesan mixture and coat all over, pressing the crumbs on to the lamb.

2 racks of French-trimmed lamb, about 625 g (1¼ lb) total weight

3. Roast the lamb in a preheated oven, 200°C (400°C), Gas Mark 6, for 20 minutes.

50 g (2 oz) Parmesan, freshly grated

50 g (2 oz) fresh breadcrumbs

4. Cut the lamb into 4 pairs of cutlets and serve with lemon wedges. Garnish with flat leaf parsley and shavings of Parmesan. Baby new potatoes, carrot matchsticks and beans make good accompaniments.

2 eggs, beaten

salt and pepper

lemon wedges, to serve

To garnish:

sprigs of flat leaf parsley

Parmesan shavings

Serves 4

cheese information: Parmesan page 78

toasted edam
and garlic sausage baguette

1 large baguette

50 g (2 oz) butter, softened

1 garlic clove, crushed

8 slices of Edam

8 slices of fully cooked, smoked garlic sausage

8 slices of honey-roast ham

8 thin slices of tomato

Serves 4 as a first course;
2 as a light meal

1. Make 8 cuts across the loaf almost to the base, spacing the cuts evenly along its length.

2. Cream the butter with the crushed garlic and spread between the slices of bread. Place one slice of cheese, sausage, ham and tomato in each cut. Press gently together to reshape the loaf.

3. Cover the loaf loosely with foil and bake in a preheated oven, 190°C (375°F), Gas Mark 5, for 5–10 minutes.

4. Remove the top of the foil and bake for a further 5 minutes, or until golden. Pull the baguette apart or cut between the slices and serve immediately.

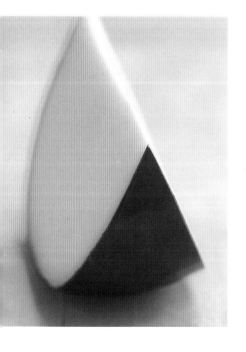

cheese information: Edam page 43

asparagus
and three-cheese pan pizza

65 g (2½ oz) tomato purée

1 garlic clove, crushed

½ teaspoon dried basil

½ teaspoon dried oregano

1 quantity Fresh Herb Dough
(see page 153)

25 g (1 oz) Mozzarella, grated

250 g (8 oz) tomatoes, skinned
and sliced

250 g (8 oz) frozen
asparagus, defrosted

75 g (3 oz) Bel Paese, cubed

1 tablespoon chopped
thyme (optional)

1 tablespoon freshly
grated Parmesan

Makes 1 x 30 cm (12 inch) pizza

1. Mix together the tomato purée, crushed garlic, basil and oregano.

2. Lightly grease a large (30 cm/12 inch) heavy-based frying pan. Roll out the dough on a floured surface to the size of the pan, then place in the pan and bring a little dough up the sides.

3. Sprinkle the grated Mozzarella over the dough and spoon the tomato purée mixture on top. Arrange the sliced tomatoes and asparagus over the pizza and sprinkle with the Bel Paese, thyme, if using, and grated Parmesan.

4. Cook over a medium heat for 15–20 minutes, then place under a preheated hot grill for 1–2 minutes, until the top is golden. Serve hot.

mozzarella and
red pesto pizza

Fresh Rosemary Dough:

250 g (8 oz) unbleached strong plain flour

1 teaspoon fast-action dried yeast

1 teaspoon salt

1 tablespoon rosemary leaves, finely chopped

1 tablespoon olive oil

125–150 ml (4–5 fl oz) warm water

Red Pesto:

1 garlic clove, crushed

25 g (1 oz) pine nuts

50 g (2 oz) sun-dried tomatoes in oil, drained and sliced

25 g (1 oz) basil leaves

75 ml (3 fl oz) extra virgin olive oil

2 tablespoons freshly grated Parmesan

salt and pepper

Topping:

125 g (4 oz) Mozzarella, diced

125 g (4 oz) cherry tomatoes, halved

50 g (2 oz) pitted black olives

Makes 1 x 30 cm (12 inch) pizza

1. First make the dough. Sift the flour, yeast and salt into a bowl. Make a well in the centre and add the chopped rosemary and oil. Gradually pour in the warm water; stir vigorously, drawing in the flour a little at a time, to form a soft dough. Knead the dough for at least 10 minutes, until it feels smooth and springy. Transfer to an oiled bowl, turning once to coat the dough with the oil. Cover the bowl with a clean tea towel and leave to rise in a warm place for 1–2 hours, until doubled in size.

2. To make the red pesto, place the garlic, pine nuts, sun-dried tomatoes and basil in a blender or food processor and process until fairly smooth. (Alternatively, grind using a pestle and mortar.) Gradually beat in the extra virgin olive oil, then stir in the grated Parmesan. Taste and season with salt and pepper, if necessary.

3. When the dough has risen, knock it back and turn it out on to a lightly floured surface. Knead again briefly for 2–3 minutes. Roll out the dough to a 30 cm (12 inch) round and place on a greased baking sheet.

4. Spread the red pesto over the pizza dough and sprinkle with the diced Mozzarella. Arrange the cherry tomatoes and olives on the top and bake in a preheated oven, 200°C (400°F), Gas Mark 6, for 20 minutes. Serve hot.

cheese information: Mozzarella page 73; Parmesan page 78

smoked haddock
and gruyère pizza

Fresh Herb Dough:

**250 g (8 oz) unbleached strong
plain flour**

1 teaspoon fast-action dried yeast

1 teaspoon salt

1 tablespoon finely chopped herbs

1 tablespoon olive oil

125-150 ml (4–5 fl oz) warm water

Tomato Sauce:

3 tablespoons olive oil

400 g (13 oz) can chopped tomatoes

1 teaspoon dried oregano

pinch of sugar

salt and pepper

Topping:

**300 g (10 oz) smoked haddock fillet,
poached and flaked**

2 tablespoons chopped parsley

3 spring onions, finely chopped

50 g (2 oz) pitted black olives

125 g (4 oz) Gruyère, grated

Makes 1 x 30 cm (12 inch) pizza

1. First make the dough. Sift the flour, yeast and salt into a bowl. Make a well in the centre and add the chopped herbs and oil. Gradually pour in the warm water; stir vigorously, drawing in the flour a little at a time, to form a soft dough. Knead the dough for at least 10 minutes, until it feels smooth and springy. Transfer to an oiled bowl, turning once to coat the dough with the oil. Cover the bowl with a clean tea towel and leave to rise in a warm place for 1–2 hours, until doubled in size.

2. Meanwhile, make the tomato sauce. Put all the sauce ingredients in a saucepan and bring to the boil. Simmer briskly, uncovered, for 20–25 minutes, until the sauce is very thick. Season to taste.

3. Knock back the dough and turn it out on to a lightly floured surface. Knead again briefly for 2–3 minutes. Roll out the dough to a 30 cm (12 inch) round, making the edge slightly thicker than the rest, and place on a greased baking sheet.

4. Spread the tomato sauce over the pizza base and sprinkle over the flaked haddock. Season with salt and pepper. Scatter over the parsley, spring onions and olives. Top the pizza with the grated Gruyère and bake in a preheated oven, 200°C (400°F), Gas Mark 6, for 20 minutes. Serve hot.

broad bean, pancetta
and fontina risotto

3 tablespoons olive oil

1 onion, finely chopped

3 garlic cloves, crushed

75 g (3 oz) pancetta, chopped

250 g (8 oz) arborio rice

½ teaspoon dried mixed herbs

900 ml (1½ pints) hot chicken or
vegetable stock

125 g (4 oz) broad beans,
defrosted if frozen

75 g (3 oz) peas

75 g (3 oz) Fontina, coarsely grated

50 g (2 oz) butter

2 tablespoons freshly grated
Parmesan, plus extra shavings
to serve

1 tablespoon chopped mint leaves

6–8 basil leaves, shredded, plus
extra to serve

salt and pepper

Serves 4 as a first course;
2 as a main course

An everyday Italian cheese, Fontina is used here with Parmesan to give a good flavour to this broad bean risotto. Serve the risotto with a drizzle of extra virgin olive oil and a few olives, accompanied by a glass of good red wine.

1. Heat the olive oil in a large pan and fry the onion until softened. Add the crushed garlic and pancetta to the pan and fry until the pancetta is golden brown. Add the rice and stir the grains into the onion mixture to coat in the olive oil.

2. With the pan still over a medium heat, add the dried mixed herbs and the hot stock to the rice and bring the mixture to the boil, stirring constantly. Season with salt and pepper and reduce to a simmer. Simmer for 10 minutes, stirring frequently. Add the broad beans and peas to the pan and continue to cook for a further 10 minutes.

3. Remove the pan from the heat and stir the grated Fontina through the risotto. Dot the butter on top together with the grated Parmesan. Cover the pan with a lid and leave aside for 2–3 minutes to allow the cheese and butter to melt into the risotto.

4. Remove the lid and add the chopped mint and shredded basil and gently stir the cheese, butter and herbs through the risotto. Serve immediately with fresh basil leaves and extra shavings of Parmesan.

cheese information: Fontina page 47; Parmesan page 78

penne with parmesan
and walnut sauce

2 litres (3½ pints) boiling water

500–750 g (1–1½ lb) dried
penne rigate

300 ml (½ pint) milk

2 slices of wholemeal bread,
crusts removed

300 g (10 oz) walnut pieces

1 garlic clove, crushed

50 g (2 oz) Parmesan, freshly
grated, plus extra to serve

100 ml (3½ fl oz) olive oil

150 ml (¼ pint) double cream

salt and pepper

Serves 4–6

1. Pour the boiling water into a large saucepan. Add a pinch of salt and bring back to the boil. Cook the pasta for 8–12 minutes, or according to the packet instructions.

2. Meanwhile, pour the milk into a shallow dish and soak the bread slices in the milk until all of the milk has been absorbed.

3. Meanwhile, spread the walnut pieces on a baking sheet and toast in a preheated oven, 190°C (375°F), Gas Mark 5, for 5 minutes. Set aside to cool.

4. Put the soaked bread, walnut pieces, garlic, Parmesan and olive oil in a blender or food processor and work until smooth. Season to taste with salt and pepper, then stir in the double cream.

5. Drain the cooked pasta well. Toss it in the walnut sauce and serve immediately, sprinkled with extra freshly grated Parmesan.

fettuccine with gorgonzola

2 litres (3½ pints) boiling water

500 g (1 lb) dried fettuccine or other ribbon pasta

25 g (1 oz) butter, plus extra to serve

250 g (8 oz) Gorgonzola, crumbled

150 ml (¼ pint) double cream

2 tablespoons dry vermouth

1 teaspoon cornflour

2 tablespoons chopped sage, plus extra leaves to garnish

salt and pepper

Serves 4

1. Pour the boiling water into a large saucepan. Add a pinch of salt and bring back to the boil. Cook the pasta for 8–12 minutes, or according to the packet instructions.

2. Meanwhile, melt the butter in a heavy-based saucepan. Sprinkle in the crumbled Gorgonzola and stir over a very gentle heat for 2–3 minutes, until the cheese has melted.

3. Pour in the cream and vermouth and add the cornflour, whisking well to amalgamate. Stir in the chopped sage. Cook, whisking all the time, until the sauce boils and thickens. Taste the sauce and season with salt and pepper. Set aside.

4. Drain the cooked pasta well and toss with a little butter. Reheat the sauce gently, whisking well. Pour it over the pasta and mix well. Serve immediately, garnished with extra sage leaves.

cheese information: Gorgonzola page 54

lasagne marinara

9 sheets of ready-to-cook lasagne

2 eggs, beaten

200 g (7 oz) Cheddar, grated

sprigs of dill, to garnish

Sauce:

50 g (2 oz) butter

50 g (2 oz) plain flour

600 ml (1 pint) milk

a few saffron strands

2–3 tablespoons boiling water

250 g (8 oz) salmon tail, bones removed and cut into bite-sized pieces

125 g (4 oz) cod fillet, bones removed and cut into bite-sized pieces

125 g (4 oz) squid rings

salt and pepper

Serves 4

1. Begin by making the sauce. Melt the butter in a saucepan, stir in the flour and cook for 1 minute. Gradually add the milk, whisking or beating the sauce over a moderate heat until it thickens. Pound the saffron strands to a powder in a bowl and stir in the boiling water until dissolved. Add to the white sauce, with salt and pepper to taste.

2. Fold the pieces of fish into the sauce with the squid rings. Remove from the heat.

3. Spoon one-third of the fish mixture over the base of a 1.8 litre (3 pint) ovenproof dish, then cover with a layer of lasagne sheets. Repeat these layers twice more, finishing with a layer of pasta sheets.

4. Beat the eggs and grated cheese together in a bowl. Add salt and pepper to taste and pour over the top of the lasagne.

5. Bake in a preheated oven, 190°C (375°F), Gas Mark 5, for 45 minutes, covering the dish with foil after 30 minutes if the surface starts to overbrown. Serve, garnished with sprigs of dill.

cheese information: Cheddar page 32

spinach lasagne
baked with cheese sauce

500–750 g (1–1½ lb) fresh spinach, cleaned and chopped, or 375 g (12 oz) frozen leaf spinach

1½ tablespoons olive oil

2 onions, finely chopped

2 garlic cloves, finely chopped

10 sheets of ready-to-cook lasagne

salt and pepper

Cheese Sauce:

50 g (2 oz) butter or margarine

50 g (2 oz) flour

750 ml (1¼ pints) milk

1–2 eggs (optional)

175 g (6 oz) Gruyère or Cheddar, grated

2–3 tablespoons freshly grated Parmesan

1 teaspoon prepared English mustard

Serves 4

1. Put the fresh spinach in a large saucepan and cook gently with just the water left on the leaves after rinsing; add salt and pepper to taste. Drain thoroughly, then chop finely. Cook frozen spinach as instructed on the packet.

2. Heat the olive oil in a saucepan, add the onions and garlic and cook until tender. Mix with the cooked spinach and set aside.

3. To make the cheese sauce, heat the butter or margarine in a saucepan. Stir in the flour, then gradually add the milk. Bring to the boil, then stir or whisk into a smooth sauce.

4. Beat the eggs well, if using, then whisk into the hot, but not boiling sauce. Do not reheat. Stir most of the grated cheese into the sauce, with the prepared mustard and salt and pepper to taste.

5. Make layers of lasagne, spinach and sauce in an ovenproof dish, beginning with lasagne and ending with lasagne and a coating of cheese sauce.

6. Sprinkle the remaining grated Gruyère or Cheddar and Parmesan over the top of the lasagne and bake for 25–30 minutes in a preheated oven, 190°C (375°F), Gas Mark 5. Serve hot.

cheese information: Gruyère page 57; Cheddar page 32; Parmesan 78

tomato and
aubergine parmigiana

1 large aubergine

olive oil, for frying

500 g (1 lb) ripe plum tomatoes, cut into wedges

50 g (2 oz) Parmesan, freshly grated

salt and pepper

sprigs of flat leaf parsley, to garnish

Serves 4

1. Cut the aubergine into 3 mm (⅛ inch) slices. Sprinkle with salt and place in a colander to drain for 30 minutes. Rinse well and pat the slices dry with kitchen paper.

2. Heat the olive oil in a frying pan and fry the aubergine slices in batches until golden brown. Drain on kitchen paper.

3. Arrange the tomato wedges and the fried aubergine slices in alternate layers in a shallow ovenproof dish, with a sprinkling of grated Parmesan between each layer. Season with salt and pepper.

4. Bake in a preheated oven, 190°C (375°F), Gas Mark 5, for 15–20 minutes, until browned and bubbling.

5. To serve, either allow to cool slightly and serve warm, or leave to cool completely and serve at room temperature. Garnish with parsley and serve with pasta, if liked.

cheese information: Parmesan page 78

cambozola with
campanelli and walnuts

1.8 litres (3 pints) boiling water

2 tablespoons olive oil

300 g (10 oz) dried egg campanelli

2 garlic cloves, crushed

3 tablespoons ready-made
red pesto

300 ml (½ pint) double cream

125 g (4 oz) Cambozola, crumbled

125 g (4 oz) walnuts, halved

2 tablespoons chopped basil

salt and pepper

Serves 4

1. Pour the boiling water into a large saucepan. Add a dash of the oil and a pinch of salt and bring back to the boil. Cook the pasta for about 8–12 minutes, or according to the packet instructions, until just tender.

2. Meanwhile, heat 1 tablespoon of the remaining oil in a saucepan. Fry the garlic over a gentle heat for 3 minutes, until softened. Remove from the heat. Cool slightly, then stir in the red pesto and cream.

3. Drain the pasta well and return it to the cleaned saucepan. Add the cream mixture with the cheese and walnuts. Toss to mix, then add salt and pepper to taste. Add the basil, toss again and serve. A tossed leaf salad makes an excellent accompaniment.

cheese information: Cambozola page 26

focaccia sandwich with
griddled vegetables and mozzarella

This sandwich makes a meal in itself. It can be prepared in advance, then wrapped in clingfilm and eaten on the move. Provolone would make a tasty substitute.

2 red peppers

1 small aubergine, sliced

2 courgettes, sliced lengthways

1 red onion, sliced into rings

1 loaf of focaccia

1 garlic clove, halved (optional)

150 g (5 oz) Mozzarella, sliced

75 g (3 oz) rocket

olive oil, for drizzling

sea salt and pepper

Serves 4

1. Heat a griddle pan and griddle the red peppers, whole, until the skins are charred. Set aside to cool.

2. Next, griddle the aubergine, courgettes and red onion for about 5 minutes, turning occasionally. Leave to cool.

3. Cut the focaccia in half horizontally and place each half on the griddle to lightly toast. Rub the cut edges of the garlic, if using, all over the toasted bread. Place the sliced Mozzarella on the base of the toasted focaccia.

4. Peel and discard the skin from the cooled griddled peppers and deseed. Chop the flesh roughly.

5. Layer the griddled vegetables evenly on top of the Mozzarella. Start with the aubergine, then add the courgettes, red peppers, onion and the rocket. Season each layer as you arrange it.

6. Finally, drizzle a little olive oil over the vegetables, season and place the top of the focaccia bread on top of the vegetables. Push together gently but firmly. Cut into 4 even-sized pieces and serve.

4 aubergines, about 250 g (8 oz) each, thinly sliced lengthways

olive oil, for brushing

250 g (8 oz) Ricotta

250 g (8 oz) soft goats' cheese

150 g (5 oz) Parmesan, freshly grated, plus extra shavings to serve

4 tablespoons chopped basil

4 large pieces of sun-dried tomato in oil, drained and sliced

snipped chives or sprigs of basil, to garnish

Tomato Sauce:

2 tablespoons olive oil

1 onion, chopped

2 garlic cloves, crushed

1 kg (2 lb) sun-ripened tomatoes, skinned, deseeded and chopped

150 ml (¼ pint) vegetable or chicken stock, medium dry white wine or water

about 1 tablespoon sun-dried tomato purée

salt and pepper

Serves 6–8 as a first course; 4 as a main course

The 'cannelloni' are formed from slices of aubergine cut lengthways. They are filled with a simple, light mixture of soft goats' cheese and Ricotta flavoured with basil, then served on a bed of diced peppers and rocket with a tomato sauce, to make a dish that is tasty and satisfying without being too heavy.

1. To make the tomato sauce, heat the oil in a saucepan, add the onion and cook gently, stirring occasionally, until soft. Stir in the garlic, tomatoes, stock, wine or water, and tomato purée, then simmer until thickened to a fairly light sauce. Season to taste.

2. Meanwhile, brush the aubergine slices lightly with oil. Cook under a preheated grill until evenly browned on both sides. Drain on kitchen paper.

3. Mix together the ricotta and goats' cheeses and 125 g (4 oz) of the Parmesan, the chopped basil and seasoning to taste. Spoon cheese mixture along each aubergine slice and add a sun-dried tomato slice. Roll the aubergine slices, from the short end, around the filling. Place the rolls, seam-side down, in a single layer in a shallow ovenproof dish and sprinkle with the remaining Parmesan. Place under a preheated grill for 5 minutes, until the filling is hot. Reheat the tomato sauce if necessary.

4. Serve the 'cannelloni' on warmed serving plates. Scatter over shavings of Parmesan and garnish with snipped chives or sprigs of basil. Serve the tomato sauce separately.

cheese information: Chèvre page 35; Ricotta page 88; Parmesan page 78

aubergine
cannelloni

paneer makhani

3 tablespoons vegetable oil

300 g (10 oz) Paneer, cut into thick pieces

2 large sweet onions, finely chopped

2 garlic cloves, crushed

2.5 cm (1 inch) piece of fresh root ginger, finely chopped

1 teaspoon each ground coriander, cumin, turmeric and garam masala

2 teaspoons chilli powder

½ teaspoon black mustard seeds

125 g (4 oz) dried green or brown lentils, soaked overnight, rinsed and drained

200 g (7 oz) can chopped tomatoes

1.2 litres (2 pints) vegetable stock or water

150 ml (¼ pint) Greek or thick set yogurt

2 tablespoons roughly chopped coriander, plus extra leaves to garnish

salt and pepper

Serves 4

Paneer is the 'tofu' of India – a great favourite among the vegetarian population. It is cooked in many guises – in hot curry sauces, over the open fire on kebab sticks or simply with a sabji of mixed vegetables. This mix of Paneer and lentils in a lightly spiced sauce can accompany chappati or plain boiled rice. Serve with mango chutney if liked.

1. Heat the oil in a large saucepan and fry the Paneer pieces for 1–2 minutes, or until golden brown. Remove from the oil and drain on kitchen paper.

2. Add the onions to the oil and cook slowly until caramelized and golden brown. Add the garlic, ginger and spices to the hot pan and cook, stirring well, for 2–3 minutes, or until the mustard seeds begin to pop. Add the green or brown lentils to the pan and coat in the oil.

3. Add the chopped tomatoes, vegetable stock or water to the pan and bring to the boil. Boil rapidly for 10 minutes, then cover, reduce the heat and simmer for 30 minutes, adding extra water if the sauce becomes too thick.

4. When the lentils are cooked and tender, season the sauce with salt and pepper to taste. Add the pieces of fried Paneer and the yogurt to the tomato and lentil sauce, remove from the heat and gently stir together. Cover with a lid and leave to stand for 10 minutes. Stir in the roughly chopped coriander and serve topped with extra fresh coriander leaves.

1 onion, finely chopped

1 green chilli, deseeded and finely chopped, plus extra to serve

10 eggs, beaten

1 sweetcorn cob, kernels removed or 4 tablespoons canned sweetcorn

25 g (1 oz) butter

75 g (3 oz) Manchego, crumbled, plus extra shavings to serve

1 tablespoon chopped coriander, plus extra to serve

8 flour tortillas, warmed in the oven

snipped chives, to garnish

Sweet Chilli Sauce:

4 red chillies, deseeded and finely chopped

50 g (2 oz) granulated sugar

2 tablespoons white wine vinegar

6 tablespoons water

2 tablespoons lemon juice

4½ tablespoon chopped coriander

salt and pepper

Serves 4

Manchego is used here in South American tortilla wraps with scrambled eggs jazzed up with spiced sweetcorn, shavings of extra Manchego and a sweet chilli sauce. If time is limited, opt for a bottled chilli sauce instead or a tub of the best guacamole you can find with extra chopped tomato mixed in. Serve with roasted tomatoes.

1. Begin by making the chilli sauce. Place the chopped red chillies, sugar, vinegar and water in a saucepan and heat gently until the sugar has dissolved. Bring to the boil, reduce the heat and cook for a further 10 minutes, or until it becomes a thick syrupy sauce. Remove from the heat, cool and stir in salt and pepper to taste, the lemon juice and chopped coriander.

2. To make the scrambled eggs, mix the chopped onion and the green chilli into the beaten eggs, together with the sweetcorn kernels. Season well with salt and pepper.

3. Melt the butter in a large pan and when hot, add the egg mixture. Stirring constantly, cook over a medium heat until the eggs are softly scrambled. Immediately remove from the heat and stir in the crumbled Manchego and the chopped coriander. Serve immediately on warm tortillas with slices of green chilli, fresh coriander and chives, plus extra shavings of Manchego and the sweet chilli sauce.

cheese information: Manchego page 68

scrambled eggs

and manchego in tortillas
with sweet chilli sauce

potato cakes with
monterey jack and bacon

Good wholesome, home cooking. Fried green tomatoes would finish the dish completely but unless you grow your own tomatoes, they can prove too difficult to hunt down. The cherry tomatoes used here work equally well. Fuit juice as an accompaniment is all that is required to start the day.

7–10 tablespoons vegetable oil

6 spring onions, finely chopped

750 g (1½ lb) floury potatoes, such as Estima or Maris Piper, peeled

25 g (1 oz) butter

1 small egg, beaten

125 g (4 oz) Monterey Jack or strong Cheddar, coarsely grated

handful of chives, snipped, plus extra to garnish

flour, for dusting

50 g (2 oz) dry white breadcrumbs

8 thick rashers of smoked bacon

12–16 cherry tomatoes

salt and pepper

Serves 4

1. Heat 2 tablespoons of the oil in a large saucepan. Quickly fry the spring onions until softened. Add the potatoes and enough water to cover. Add a pinch of salt and bring to the boil. Boil until tender and most of the water has evaporated (although you may need to add extra water while boiling the potatoes, as and when required). Drain well and return to the pan. Mash with the butter to make a rough texture. Set aside to cool.

2. Mix the beaten egg and half of the grated cheese into the mashed potatoes with plenty of salt and pepper and the snipped chives.

3. Divide the mixture into 8 and, with floured hands, shape the potato into small patties. Flour lightly and then coat lightly in the breadcrumbs.

4. Heat the remaining oil in a large frying pan until very hot. Cook the patties, 4 at a time, on both sides for 2–3 minutes, or until golden brown and heated through.

5. Remove the patties from the frying pan and place on a baking sheet. Sprinkle the tops of the patties with the remaining cheese and keep hot in the bottom of a preheated grill while cooking the remaining patties and the bacon and tomatoes.

6. Grill the bacon rashers and cherry tomatoes until the bacon is golden brown and crisp and the tomatoes have just burst their skins.

7. Serve the potato cakes topped with the rashers of bacon and with the cherry tomatoes. Garnish with chives and serve immediately.

swedish potato, anchovy
and cheese temptation

750 g (1½ lb) large potatoes

2 tablespoons vegetable oil

2 large onions, finely chopped

200 g (7 oz) canned anchovies, sprats or sardines, drained

75 g (3 oz) Grevé, grated

25 g (1 oz) butter, melted

1 tablespoon chopped parsley

3 tablespoons dry white breadcrumbs

150 ml (¼ pint) double cream

pepper

sprigs of chervil, to garnish

Serves 4

Totally and utterly Swedish, this dish is known to many as 'Janssen's Temptation' – except that this version also includes one of Sweden's best-known cheeses, Grevé. It is ideal cold weather food – for when you've been working hard or come fresh off the ski slopes. Serve piping hot with green salad leaves and plenty of crusty bread to mop up the juices.

1. Peel and thinly slice the potatoes. Then cut the potatoes into strips and immerse in a bowl of cold water to keep them from discolouring.

2. Heat the oil in a pan, then fry the onion until softened and beginning to brown. Place an even layer of potatoes at the bottom of a lightly buttered ovenproof dish, then a layer of fish, followed by fried onion and then another layer of potatoes. Repeat the layers, finishing with a layer of the cheese, the melted butter and then finally a layer of potatoes.

3. Sprinkle the top of the dish with black pepper, chopped parsley and the breadcrumbs. Cook on the middle shelf of a preheated oven, 220°C (425°F), Gas Mark 7, for 30 minutes.

4. Pour the cream over the top of the bake and return to the oven for a further 25 minutes. Serve straight from the oven, garnished with chervil sprigs.

cheese information: Grevé page 56

skillet potatoes and
onions with taleggio and sage

Simply, wholesome Californian cooking at its best – and using the best. The potatoes are important, so do choose the right type. Cook the dish long and slowly, and add the cheese right at the end, just as you are ready to serve. The cheese should be just melted and not over-cooked to rubber. This makes an ideal supper dish for a casual meal with friends.

4 tablespoons olive oil

25 g (1 oz) butter

4 red onions, sliced

250 g (8 oz) new or small waxy salad potatoes, such as Charlotte, unpeeled

2 garlic cloves, thinly sliced

10–12 sage leaves

2 tablespoons black olives

1/2 tablespoon thyme leaves

175 g (6 oz) Taleggio, sliced

salt and pepper

sprigs of flat leaf parsley, to garnish

Serves 4

1. Heat the olive oil and butter in a large frying pan. Add the sliced red onions and cook gently for at least 15 minutes, until caramelized. Remove from the pan and set aside.

2. Slice the potatoes evenly and add to the hot pan. Cook on both sides until golden brown – you may need to add extra olive oil.

3. Return the onions to the pan with the sliced garlic. Season well with salt and pepper. Add the sage leaves to the pan and carefully toss together.

4. Spread the potatoes out in an even layer, reduce the heat, cover the pan with a lid and cook gently for 20 minutes, turning occasionally.

5. Add the black olives and thyme leaves to the pan and the slices of Taleggio.

6. Return the pan to the heat, cover once again and cook for a further 2–3 minutes, or until the cheese has just melted. Season with plenty of black pepper. Take the pan to the table and serve piping hot, garnished with flat leaf parsley.

cheese information: Taleggio page 95

griddled beetroot, feta
and trevise salad

A member of the chicory family, trevise (radicchio di Treviso) has a very slightly bitter taste. If you cannot find trevise, use chicory or rocket instead.

500 g (1 lb) raw beetroot, peeled and cut into 1 cm (½ inch) thick slices

1 large head of trevise or 250 g (8 oz) trevise leaves

1 tablespoon red wine vinegar

2 tablespoons extra virgin olive oil

1 bunch of flat leaf parsley, chopped

250 g (8 oz) Feta, crumbled

sea salt and pepper

Serves 4

1. Heat a griddle pan. Place the beetroot slices on the griddle and cook on each side for 4–5 minutes. Place in a large bowl.

2. Cut the trevise into wedges, remove the hard core and place on the griddle to cook until just wilted, then remove and add to the beetroot.

3. Add the vinegar, olive oil and chopped parsley to the beetroot and trevise. Season to taste and toss well. Place in a serving dish, scatter the crumbled Feta over the top and serve.

cheese information: Feta page 47

griddled haloumi
with tomato salad

1. Heat a griddle pan. Cut the Haloumi into 16 slices and place on the griddle to cook for 3–4 minutes on each side.

2. Arrange the salad leaves on 4 serving plates.

500 g (1 lb) Haloumi

3. Mix together the olive oil, lemon juice and marjoram, and season to taste with salt and pepper.

1 bag of mixed salad leaves

2 tablespoons olive oil

4. Arrange the griddled Haloumi and the tomato wedges alternately on the salad leaves. Add the olives, if using, and spoon over the dressing. Serve immediately, while the cheese is still warm.

4 tablespoons lemon juice

1 bunch of marjoram, chopped

4 beef tomatoes, skinned, cored and cut into wedges

75 g (3 oz) pitted olives (optional)

sea salt and pepper

Serves 4

goats' cheese preserved
in rosemary and pepper oil

600 ml (1 pint) extra virgin olive oil

1 tablespoon mixed peppercorns

1 strip of lemon rind

2 sprigs of rosemary

2 bay leaves

250 g (8 oz) small rounds of goats' cheese

Serves 8–10

Preserved goats' cheese is ideal for grilling and serving on a thick croûte of bread with a handful of salad leaves dressed with a balsamic vinaigrette (illustrated right). Alternatively, serve the goats' cheese drizzled with the preserving olive oil as part of an antipasti or mezze menu, together with air-dried hams, olives and sun-dried tomatoes. The flavoured oil is tasty drizzled over salads.

1. Place the olive oil, peppercorns, lemon rind, rosemary and bay leaves in a saucepan and heat gently until just warm. Remove from the heat and leave to stand until cold. Remove the lemon rind, rosemary and bay leaves and set aside.

2. Pack the goats' cheeses, lemon rind, rosemary and bay leaves into a large clean jar. Pour the olive oil and peppercorns into the jar over the goats' cheeses.

3. Add enough olive oil so that the cheese is completely covered with oil and there is preferably a 2.5 cm (1 inch) layer of oil on top. Tap the jar to remove any air bubbles and to settle the goats' cheese, herbs and spices. (The oil acts as an airtight seal and will keep the goats' cheese fresh.)

4. Seal the jar tightly and leave in a cool dark place or in the fridge for up to 2 weeks.

cheese information: Chèvre page 35

radicchio and orange
salad with brie

Dates make a delicious addition to this combination of salad leaves, citrus fruit and Brie.

1. Using a zester, remove small strips of rind from 1 of the oranges. Set aside. Using a small sharp knife, peel the rind and pith from both oranges. Slice the flesh firmly.

2 small oranges

1 head of radicchio, roughly torn

1 bunch of watercress or handful of rocket

250 g (8 oz) fresh dates, pitted and chopped

175 g (6 oz) Brie, rind removed, and diced

6 tablespoons Sweet Mustard Dressing (see opposite) or ready-made French dressing

salt and pepper

Serves 4

2. Arrange all the salad ingredients in a serving bowl or on individual plates. Scatter the reserved orange rind over the top. Season with salt and pepper. Drizzle the dressing over the salad just before serving.

cheese information: Brie page 22

cabbage, apple
and wensleydale salad

50 g (2 oz) pecans or walnuts,
roughly chopped

1 small red cabbage,
finely shredded

1 red or white onion, thinly sliced

175 g (6 oz) fresh dates, pitted and
roughly chopped

1 large red apple, cored, halved and
thinly sliced

150 g (5 oz) Wensleydale, crumbled

salt and pepper

Sweet Mustard Dressing:

3 tablespoons olive oil

2 tablespoons wholegrain mustard

1 tablespoon clear honey

1 teaspoon white wine vinegar
or lemon juice

Serves 4–6;
dressing makes 75 ml (3 fl oz)

1. Place the pecans or walnuts on a baking sheet and toast under a preheated hot grill for 2–3 minutes, until browned. Set aside.

2. Place the cabbage in a large salad bowl with the onion, dates and apple. Season with salt and pepper and toss lightly to mix.

3. To make the dressing, place all the ingredients in a small bowl and whisk with a balloon whisk until thoroughly blended. Alternatively, place all the ingredients in a screw-top jar, close the lid tightly and shake until thoroughly combined.

4. Scatter the crumbled Wensleydale over the salad and sprinkle over the reserved toasted nuts. Drizzle the mustard dressing over the top and serve at once.

This is Mediterranean cooking at its best. Cooked in a crisp shell of filo pastry, the pie makes an ideal picnic or summer recipe. It is easy to transport and keeps well for a few days.

(1¹/₂ lb) fresh spinach leaves, cleaned

250 g (8 oz) Feta, roughly crumbled

¹/₂ teaspoon dried chilli flakes

75 g (3 oz) Parmesan, finely grated

50 g (2 oz) pine nuts, toasted

15 g (¹/₂ oz) dill, chopped

15 g (¹/₂ oz) tarragon, chopped

3 eggs, beaten

1 teaspoon grated nutmeg

250 g (8 oz) fresh filo pastry

5–8 tablespoons olive oil

1 tablespoon sesame seeds

salt and pepper

Serves 6

1. Put the spinach in a large saucepan with just the water left on the leaves after rinsing. Cook gently until wilted and soft. Drain well. When cooled slightly wring all of the water out of the leaves. (This is easiest done wearing washing-up gloves.)

2. Mix the Feta into the spinach with the chilli flakes, Parmesan, pine nuts and herbs. Add the beaten eggs to the mixture along with plenty of salt, pepper and grated nutmeg. Combine together well.

3. Unwrap the filo pastry and, working quickly, brush the top sheet of pastry with a little olive oil. (While working, keep the stack of filo pastry covered with a clean tea towel to prevent it from drying out.) Lay the sheet in the bottom of a lightly greased 20 cm (8 inch) loose-bottomed cake tin with the edges overlapping the rim of the tin. Brush the next sheet of pastry and lay it in the opposite direction to the first sheet to completely cover the base of the tin. Repeat this brushing with oil and layering in the tin until at least 6–8 sheets of pastry have created a shell and there are at least 3 sheets of pastry left for a 'lid'.

4. Spoon the spinach mixture into the filo pastry shell, pushing it in well with the back of the spoon and levelling the surface.

5. Brush the next sheet of pastry with oil and then cut the length of the remaining stack of filo pastry into 5 cm (2 inch) wide strips. One by one, place these strips of pastry over the top of the spinach in a casual folded arrangement, remembering to brush all the strips of pastry with oil.

6. Once all the strips are in place, fold in the over-hanging filo towards the middle. Sprinkle with sesame seeds and bake in a preheated oven, 190°C (375°F), Gas Mark 5, for 1 hour. Remove from the oven, leave to cool for 15 minutes, then gently push the pie up and out of the tin. Serve warm or cold.

cheese information: Feta page 47; Parmesan page 78

spinach and feta
filo pie with pine nuts

hazelnut and
gorgonzola quiche

50 g (2 oz) butter

1 tablespoon vegetable oil

2 large leeks, thinly sliced

150 ml (¼ pint) whipping cream

150ml (¼ pint) milk

2 tablespoons chopped
flat leaf parsley

2 eggs, beaten

125 g (4 oz) Gorgonzola, crumbled

75 g (3 oz) whole hazelnuts,
lightly toasted

salt and pepper

Cheese Pastry:

250 g (8 oz) plain flour

pinch of salt

pinch of cayenne pepper

75 g (3 oz) butter

25 g (1 oz) Cheddar, finely grated

6–8 tablespoons cold water

Serves 6–8

Rich and creamy, this tart is packed with leeks and the distinctive flavour of Gorgonzola. Cooked until just set, it is topped with a layer of toasted whole hazelnuts for extra crunch and a mellow nutty thrill.

1. To make the cheese pastry, put the flour, salt and cayenne pepper in a blender or food processor with the butter and work to fine breadcrumbs. Add the grated Cheddar and mix together. Add the cold water and combine the ingredients to a soft, pliable pastry. Wrap in clingfilm and chill for 1 hour.

2. Roll out the pastry on a lightly floured surface and use to line a 20 cm (8 inch) deep flan tin. Prick the base with a fork and chill for 1 hour. Bake blind (see page 192) in a preheated oven, 190°C (375°F), Gas Mark 5, for 12 minutes. Remove the paper and baking beans and bake for a further 5 minutes.

3. To make the quiche filling, heat the butter and oil in a large frying pan and fry the sliced leeks until softened and caramelized. Remove from the heat and allow to cool.

4. Beat the cream, milk, chopped parsley and eggs together. Stir the egg mixture into the caramelized leeks and season well with salt and pepper. Stir the crumbled Gorgonzola into the mixture, then pour it into the cooked pastry shell. Smooth the surface, then scatter the hazelnuts over the top.

5. Bake the quiche on the middle shelf of the oven for 40–50 minutes, or until the egg mixture has just set in the middle. Remove from the oven and allow to cool slightly before serving with a mixed green salad.

munster, red pepper
and chive tartlets

These tartlets are garlicky with a strong cheese accent. Munster goes well with the caramelized red onions and pungent flavour of chives. Make them mini-sized for canapés or picnic fare or scale up and cook the same quantity in a 20 cm (8 inch) flan tin for about 35 minutes, or until the centre is firm.

400 g (13 oz) shortcrust pastry, defrosted if frozen

1 tablespoon vegetable oil

15 g (½ oz) butter

1 red onion, finely chopped

1 small red pepper, roasted, peeled and thinly sliced

150 ml (¼ pint) single cream

2 eggs

2 garlic cloves, crushed

15 g (½ oz) chives, snipped

75 g (3 oz) Munster, roughly chopped

salt and pepper

basil leaves, to garnish

Serves 4

1. Roll out the pastry on a lightly floured surface and use to line 4 x 10 cm (4 inch) tartlet tins. Prick the bases, line with circles of greaseproof paper and fill with baking beans, then chill for 30 minutes.

2. Place the tartlets on a baking sheet and bake blind in a preheated oven, 190°C (375°F), Gas Mark 5, for 8 minutes. Remove the paper and beans and bake for a further 2–3 minutes, or until the shells are crisp and beginning to brown. Remove from the oven and cool slightly.

3. Heat the oil and butter in a pan and fry the sliced red onion until caramelized. Divide the onion and the roasted red pepper strips among the pastry shells.

4. Beat the cream, eggs, salt and pepper together. Add the crushed garlic and chives to the mixture and divide it among the pastry shells. Sprinkle the Munster over the tartlets and bake on the middle shelf of the oven for 20–25 minutes, or until just cooked. Garnish with basil.

cheese information: Munster page 74

stilton and
apple strudel

Apples, walnuts and Stilton rolled together in a strudel and baked until the pastry is crisp – novel but it works. Slice and serve while still warm with salad leaves or make 2 smaller strudels and serve slices on a cheeseboard alongside other cheeses, oatcakes and pears. It would taste just as good with a large spoonful of crème fraîche – everyone would wonder whether it was savoury or sweet. You choose!

500 g (1 lb) Bramley apples, peeled, cored and chopped

2 celery sticks, finely chopped

½ teaspoon grated nutmeg

25 g (1 oz) butter

50 g (2 oz) walnuts, chopped

2 tablespoons caster sugar

125 g (4 oz) Stilton, crumbled

200 g (7 oz) fresh filo pastry

8 tablespoons olive oil

1 teaspoon sesame seeds

1 teaspoon cumin seeds

sprigs of flat leaf parsley, to garnish

Serves 6

1. Mix the apples with the celery and nutmeg.

2. Melt the butter in a large wide saucepan or frying pan. Add the walnuts and lightly toast the nuts. Add the sugar and stir together. Add the apple and celery mix, stir together and cook for a further 3 minutes. Remove from the heat and leave to cool. When cold, stir in the crumbled Stilton.

3. Unwrap the filo pastry and, working quickly, lay the top sheet of pastry on the work surface and brush with a little olive oil. (While working, keep the stack of filo pastry covered with a clean tea towel to prevent it from drying out.) Cover with a second sheet of pastry and repeat the oiling and layering with pastry. Continue until all the pastry and oil has been used.

4. Spoon most of the apple and Stilton mixture in a mound along one long edge of the pastry and sprinkle the remainder across the rest of the pastry. Roll into a strudel starting from the edge with the filling. Place the strudel on a baking sheet, seam side down, and brush with a little olive oil. Sprinkle the sesame and cumin seeds over the top and bake on the middle shelf of a preheated oven, 200°C (400°F), Gas Mark 6, for 20–25 minutes, or until golden. Remove from the oven; allow to cool before slicing thickly and serving garnished with flat leaf parsley.

cheese information: Stilton page 94

mascarpone
and date tart

150 g (5 oz) plain flour

75 g (3 oz) plus 2 tablespoons caster sugar

75 g (3 oz) butter, chilled

3 egg yolks

250 g (8 oz) fresh dates, halved and pitted

250 g (8 oz) Mascarpone

125 ml (4 fl oz) double cream

2 eggs, lightly beaten

1 tablespoon cornflour

2 teaspoons vanilla essence

Serves 8

This delightful dessert comprises soft cheese mixed with fresh dates and baked in a pastry case.

1. Combine the flour, 75 g (3 oz) of the sugar, the butter and egg yolks in a blender or food processor and work until the mixture just comes together. Turn out the mixture on a lightly floured surface and press together until smooth. Roll out the dough, between two sheets of clingfilm, until it is large enough to cover the base and sides of a greased 23 cm (9 inch) fluted flan tin. Ease the pastry into the tin and trim the edges. Chill for 20 minutes.

2. Cut a sheet of greaseproof paper to cover the bottom of the pastry case. Spread a layer of baking beans over the paper and bake blind in a preheated oven, 180°C (350°F), Gas Mark 4, for 10 minutes. Remove the paper and baking beans and cook the pastry case for another 10 minutes, until golden. Leave to cool.

3. Scatter the dates over the cooked pastry base. Combine the Mascarpone, cream, eggs, the remaining 2 tablespoons caster sugar, cornflour and vanilla essence in a bowl and whisk until smooth. Pour the mixture into the pastry case and bake for 35 minutes, or until the filling is golden and set.

cheese information: Mascarpone page 69

hot chocolate
crêpes

Crêpes:

100 g (3½ oz) plain flour

15 g (½ oz) cocoa powder

2 tablespoons caster sugar

1 egg

300 ml (½ pint) milk

vegetable oil, for frying

Filling:

1 piece of stem ginger, about 15 g (½ oz), finely chopped

2 tablespoons caster sugar

250 g (8 oz) Ricotta

50 g (2 oz) raisins

150 g (5 oz) white chocolate, finely chopped

3 tablespoons double cream

Glossy Chocolate Sauce:

125 g (4 oz) caster sugar

125 ml (4 fl oz) water

175 g (6 oz) plain chocolate, broken into pieces

25 g (1 oz) unsalted butter

Serves 4

1. To make the crêpes, sift the flour and cocoa powder into a bowl. Stir in the sugar. Add the egg and a little of the milk, and whisk to make a stiff batter. Beat in the remaining milk.

2. Heat a little oil in a medium sized frying pan. Pour off the oil. When the pan is very hot, pour in a little batter and tilt the pan so that the batter coats the base. Cook over a moderate heat until browned on the underside.

3. Flip over the crêpe with a palette knife and cook the other slide. Slide the crêpe out of the pan and keep warm. Add a little more oil to the pan and make 7 more crêpes in the same way, keeping the cooked ones warm.

4. Combine all the filling ingredients in a bowl. Place spoonfuls of the filling in the centres of the crêpes. Fold each one into quarters, enclosing the filling. Place the crêpes in a large shallow ovenproof dish. Bake in a preheated oven, 200°C (400°F), Gas Mark 6, for 10 minutes, until heated through.

5. Meanwhile, make the chocolate sauce. Heat the caster sugar and water in a small, heavy-based saucepan until the sugar has dissolved. Bring to the boil and boil for 1 minute. Remove from the heat and stir in the plain chocolate and unsalted butter. Stir until dissolved, then serve with the hot crêpes.

cheese information: Ricotta page 88

This is simplicity itself. Soft and creamy, this dessert is the perfect partner with soft fruits. New, unused small plant pots make ideal moulds or use traditional china heart-shaped moulds. If neither is available, use small teacups or ramekins, but remember the desserts may be a little wetter since the excess water has not had the opportunity to drain away.

50 g (2 oz) caster sugar

3 tablespoons water

2–3 fresh lavender flowers (optional)

1 egg white

500 g (1 lb) Quark

175 g (6 oz) crème fraîche

sprigs of mint, to decorate

Fruit Syrup:

25 g (1 oz) caster sugar

2 tablespoons water

250 g (8 oz) mixed soft fruit, such as raspberries, blueberries and blackberries

Serves 4

1. Put the caster sugar and water in a small saucepan and simmer gently until the sugar has dissolved. Add the lavender flowers to the syrup, if using, and simmer for 3 minutes. Remove from the heat and leave to cool.

2. Whisk the egg white in a clean bowl until standing in stiff peaks. Place the Quark and crème fraîche in a bowl. Stir in the cold lavender syrup, then fold in the whisked egg white.

3. Line 4 moulds with damp pieces of muslin and stand the moulds on a plate to catch the liquid that will drip out of the base of the moulds. Spoon the cheese mixture into the muslin-lined moulds, level the surface and refrigerate overnight.

4. To make the fruit syrup, put the caster sugar and water in a small saucepan and heat gently to dissolve the sugar. Add half the fruit to the warm syrup and cook for 1 minute, then remove from the heat. When the syrup and fruit are cold stir in the remaining fruit.

5. Turn the cheeses out of their moulds. Serve with the soft fruits and decorated with mint sprigs.

cheese information: Quark page 83

lavender sweet cheese
with soft fruits

tiramisu with
raspberry surprise

This dessert is best made the night before so that it can set completely.

1. Combine the coffee and grappa or brandy. Dip the sponge fingers into the liquid to coat them evenly, then arrange them in a small shallow dish or a serving platter, pouring any excess liquid over them. Sprinkle the raspberries evenly over the soaked sponge fingers.

4 tablespoons very strong espresso coffee

2. In a bowl, whisk together the Mascarpone, egg yolks and icing sugar until smooth and well blended.

2 tablespoons grappa or brandy

10 sponge fingers

3. In another bowl, whisk the egg whites until stiff and glossy, then fold into the Mascarpone mixture until well blended.

125 g (4 oz) raspberries

4. Spoon the mixture over the sponge fingers and smooth the surface. Finely grate the chocolate straight on to the mixture. Cover and chill until set. Decorate with mint leaves.

175 g (6 oz) Mascarpone

2 eggs, separated

50 g (2 oz) icing sugar

25 g (1 oz) plain chocolate

mint leaves, to decorate

Serves 4

cheese information: Mascarpone page 69

baked bananas
with mascarpone and rum cream

1–2 tablespoons caster sugar

½ teaspoon ground cinnamon

2 teaspoons rum

250 g (8 oz) Mascarpone

8 small bananas

Serves 4

1. Mix the sugar, cinnamon and rum in a bowl. Stir in the Mascarpone, mix well and set aside.

2. Place the whole unpeeled bananas on a barbecue grill over hot coals and cook for 10–12 minutes, turning the bananas as the skins darken, until they are black all over and the flesh is very tender.

3. To seve, split the bananas open and spread the flesh with the Mascarpone cream.

Note: A delicious variation is Baked Bananas with Chocolate Ricotta Cream. Mix 250 g (8 oz) Ricotta and 1–2 tablespoons maple syrup in a bowl. Stir in 15 g (½ oz) hazelnuts and beat in 50 g (2 oz) dark chocolate, melted. Prepare the baked bananas as in the main recipe and serve with the chocolate Ricotta cream. Sprinkle with 15 g (½ oz) hazelnuts.

cheese information: Mascarpone page 69; Ricotta page 88

cassata alla siciliana

500 g (1 lb) Madeira cake, cut into 1 cm (1/2 inch) thick slices

4 tablespoons Maraschino or Kirsch

500 g (1 lb) fresh Ricotta, drained and sieved

150 ml (1/4 pint) single cream

2 tablespoons sugar

1 teaspoon ground cinnamon

125 g (4 oz) plain chocolate, finely chopped

175 g (6 oz) whole mixed glacé fruits, finely chopped

2 tablespoons pistachio nuts, blanched, peeled and chopped

1/2 teaspoon orange-flower water

sifted icing sugar, for sprinkling

Serves 8

This dessert may be prepared up to 1 day in advance. Cover and chill until the point of serving.

1. Line the base and sides of a 1.8 litre (3 pint) pudding basin or ring mould with nonstick baking paper.

2. Use three-quarters of the cake slices to line the base and sides of the mould, cutting and trimming them to shape as necessary. Sprinkle 2 tablespoons of the liqueur over the cake.

3. Whip the Ricotta until creamy, then beat in the cream, sugar, cinnamon, chocolate, chopped glacé fruits and pistachio nuts. Stir in the orange-flower water. Pour this mixture into the prepared mould and smooth the top. Trim the remaining cake slices and arrange them on top. Sprinkle with the remaining liqueur. Cover and chill for 3–4 hours.

4. Carefully unmould the cake on to a serving platter and sprinkle with sifted icing sugar to serve.

cheese information: Ricotta page 88

fresh blueberry
cheesecake

1 tablespoon sugar

1 tablespoon water

250 g (8 oz) blueberries

Biscuit Base:

about 125 g (4 oz) digestive
biscuits, crushed

75 g (3 oz) caster sugar

1 teaspoon ground allspice

75 g (3 oz) butter

1½ tablespoons apricot jam

Cheese Filling:

1 tablespoon powdered gelatine

125 ml (4 fl oz) orange juice

150 g (5 oz) light brown sugar

2 tablespoons grated orange rind

425 g (14 oz) cream cheese

425 g (14 oz) Ricotta

125 ml (4 fl oz) double or
whipped cream

Serves 8

1. To make the biscuit base, mix the biscuit crumbs in a bowl with the caster sugar and allspice. Melt the butter and jam in a small saucepan, then stir into the crumb mixture. Press into the bottom and up the sides of a greased and lined 20 cm (8 inch) springform cake tin. Refrigerate.

2. Place the sugar in a saucepan with the water and heat gently to dissolve the sugar. Add half of the blueberries and simmer gently for 2 minutes. Remove from the heat and leave to cool.

3. To make the filling, dissolve the gelatine in the orange juice in a bowl set over a saucepan of simmering water. Stir in the brown sugar and orange rind. Add the cheeses and beat thoroughly. Reserve a little cream and fold the rest into the filling.

4. Strain the cooked blueberries. Spread them over the biscuit base, cover with the cheese filling, and top with the remaining fresh blueberries and cream. Chill for 5–6 hours.

cheese information: Ricotta page 88

pistou

3 garlic cloves, crushed

15 g (½ oz) basil leaves

150 ml (¼ pint) virgin olive oil

50 g (2 oz) walnuts or pine nuts

1 teaspoon lemon juice

50 g (2 oz) Parmesan, freshly grated

salt and pepper

Makes 300 ml (½ pint)

Make the pistou as and when needed, or store in the refrigerator covered with enough oil to create an airtight seal. Keep for 4–5 days. Experiment with the nuts and herbs to create new combinations. Hazelnuts or almonds pair well with basil, as well as with parsley or coriander.

1. Put the garlic in a blender or food processor or a large pestle and mortar. Add the basil leaves and blend together roughly.

2. Add the olive oil, a little at time, to make a fresh green purée. Add the walnuts or pine nuts, salt if necessary, black pepper and lemon juice. Blend together briefly.

3. Add the grated Parmesan and stir in.

cheese information: Parmesan page 78

creamy blue cheese dressing

125 g (4 oz) blue cheese, such as
Bleu d'Auvergne, Cashel Blue,
Danish Blue or Roquefort, crumbled

125 ml (4 fl oz) mayonnaise

125 ml (4 fl oz) double cream

large pinch of salt

1/2 teaspoon pepper

Makes 300 ml (½ pint)

1. Combine all the ingredients in a mixing bowl, beating until thoroughly combined. Store the dressing in the refrigerator until ready to use.

cheese information: Bleu d'Auvergne page 21; Cashel Blue page 30; Danish Blue page 40; Roquefort page 89

mornay sauce

40 g (1½ oz) butter

25 g (1 oz) plain flour

450 ml (¾ pint) milk

pinch of ground nutmeg

45 g (1¾ oz) Parmesan,
freshly grated

45 g (1¾ oz) Emmental,
freshly grated

salt and cayenne pepper

Serves 4

1. Melt 25 g (1 oz) of the butter in a small saucepan. Stir in the flour and cook gently for 1–2 minutes.

2. Add the milk, a little at a time, stirring after each addition, until totally absorbed. When all the milk has been incorporated and the sauce is smooth, season lightly with nutmeg, salt and cayenne.

3. Simmer very gently for 5 minutes, stirring occasionally to prevent the sauce from sticking to the pan. Stir in the remaining butter and the grated cheese and stir until the cheese has melted. Serve with vegetables or fish.

cheese information: Emmental page 44; Parmesan page 78

roquefort
and oil dressing

150 ml (¼ pint) olive oil

2 teaspoons salt

2 teaspoons pepper

4 tablespoons wine vinegar

**50 g (2 oz) Roquefort,
finely crumbled**

2 tablespoons snipped chives

Makes 250 ml (8 fl oz)

1. Beat the olive oil, salt and pepper together in a mixing bowl. Gradually beat in the vinegar, then stir in the crumbled Roquefort until the mixture is well combined. Stir in the chives.

2. Either use the dressing immediately or pour it into a screw-top jar and chill in the refrigerator until required.

cheese information: Roquefort page 89

danish blue dip

Serve this tasty dip with Scottish oatcakes, breadsticks or a selection of fresh vegetables, such as carrot matchsticks, cauliflower and broccoli florets.

**250 g (8 oz) Danish Blue or
Gorgonzola, softened**

350 ml (12 fl oz) double cream

1 tablespoon Worcestershire sauce

salt and pepper

Serves 4

1. Place the cheese and cream in a bowl. Mix together with a wooden spoon, then beat vigorously. Stir in the Worcestershire sauce and seasoning to taste. Spoon into a serving bowl and chill in the refrigerator before serving.

cheese information: Danish Blue page 40; Gorgonzola page 54

glossary of cheese terms

Appellation d'Origine Controllée see page 10.

Acid curd milk coagulated or fermented by lactic acid and not rennet.

Annatto permitted colouring agent (E160b) in cheese, giving characteristic orange colour found in Red Leicester or Double Gloucester. Obtained from the seeds of the *Bixa orellana* bush.

Bloom the pale, soft, downy growth found on the surface of cheeses such as Brie and Camembert.

Brine a salt solution.

Brining a process of ripening a cheese with the aid of regularly washing it with a brine solution.

Brined a cheese that is ripened in brine.

Casein the main protein in milk which solidifies during coagulation.

Cheddaring the technique where the curd is repeatedly piled and turned to drain the whey and mat together the curds until they resemble chicken breast.

Coagulation the conversion or clotting of the milk to a solid through rennet, lactic acid or heat.

Cooked cheese after coagulation, the temperature of the whey is raised effectively to cook the curds. Used in making very hard cheeses.

Culture a controlled production of micro-organisms.

Curds the solid particles formed when the junket is cut.

Curing the aging or ripening process of the cheese.

Creamery a factory where cheese is made on a large scale.

Denominacion de Origen see page 10.

Denominazione di Origine Controllatta see page 10.

Evening milk is that obtained from the evening milking and is usually richer in fat than the morning milk.

Eyes the holes that form naturally in some cheeses, Emmental for example.

Farmhouse often abused description of a cheese made on the farm as opposed to in a creamery. Many farms now operate production facilities as large and as mechanized as creameries, so beware.

Fermier the term used to describe cheese made on the farm using unpasteurized milk.

Flora the mould growth on the surface of cheeses such as Brie and Camembert.

Fresh cheese unripened cheese.

Homogenize the treatment of milk during which the fat droplets are emulsified so the cream does not separate.

Humidity atmospheric moisture level, critical in maturing cheese.

Junket a soft gel produced after the milk is renneted.

Lactation the period when a mammal produces milk.

Lactic a term frequently used to describe the aroma and flavour of milk in cheese.

Lactic acid produced when milk sours.

Lactose milk sugar.

Morning milk from the morning milking and normally lower in fat than evening milk.

Paste the interior of the cheese, the part that is normally eaten.

Pasteurization flash heating of milk to 72°C (161.6°F) for a minimum of 15 seconds in order to destroy potentially harmful bacteria.

Penicillium candidum the mould spore responsible for the surface mould on Brie and Camembert type cheeses.

Penicillium glaucum responsible for the blue veining in Gorgonzola.

Penicillium roquefortii responsible for the blue veining in Roquefort, Stilton and many other blue cheeses.

Product of Designated Origin see page 10.

Propionic acid the action during cheese ripening that creates the natural holes in cheeses such as Emmental and Gruyère.

Raw milk unpasteurized milk.

Rennet coagulant naturally produced from Chymosin (qv) or from plants or increasingly, grown from microbes (yeast or fungus) for making vegetarian cheese.

Scalding the heating of the curds so that more whey can be extracted.

Skimmed milk milk from which the cream has either been part removed (semi-skimmed) or completely removed (skimmed) to produce a lower-fat milk.

Starter a culture of lactic acid bacteria added to milk at the start of cheesemaking to increase acidity and improve flavours.

Surface ripened how cheeses mature through the action of surface mould which work their way into the cheese.

Territorial cheeses British cheeses named after the counties in which they were historically produced. Cheshire, Lancashire, Red Leicester, Gloucester, Caerphilly, Derby.

Truckle: a small cylindrical cheese, usually between 2–4.5 kg (4–10 lb) in weight.

Washed rind cheeses are bathed or washed in whey, brine, oil or alcohol during the ripening period to inhibit mould growth and produce the reddish coloured surface smears.

Whey the watery by-product released, separated or pressed from the junket or curd.

Whole milk milk with all its fat.

index

Thanks and acknowledgments to:

Jenni Muir for years of helpful advice. Sandy Carr for her extraordinarily reliable *Pocket Cheese Book*, now sadly out of print. Clarissa Hyman for some great writing over the years. Glynn Christian for sharing with me his wealth of food knowledge. My wife Linda, for her contribution to every cheese talk, tutored tasting and training seminar we have ever given.